Elements of Government Contracting

CCH®

Elements of Government Contracting

Practical Advice for Negotiating and Performing Government Contracts

Richard D. Lieberman
Karen R. O'Brien

Wolters Kluwer
Law & Business

AUSTIN   BOSTON   CHICAGO   NEW YORK   THE NETHERLANDS

PREFACE

This book combines and updates our two earlier volumes, *Elements of Contract Formation: Practical Advice on Winning Government Contracts* and *Elements of Contract Administration: Practical Advice on Performing Government Contracts*. In addition, a list of helpful Internet sites may be found at Appendix B.

As was the case in the earlier volumes, our purpose is to explain the highlights of Government contracting in understandable terms. This volume is not all inclusive, but should represent a good starting point for new Government contractors, or those seeking to enter the field and sell in this market.

We would like to dedicate this book to two individuals who have significantly influenced our work: Professors Ralph C. Nash, Jr. and John Cibinic, Jr., the pillars of the field of Government contracts. Mr. Lieberman would also like to thank his spouse, Ms. Helene R. Weisz, for being a staunch supporter and helpful critic. Ms. O'Brien would like to thank her husband, George T. DeBakey, for his support and interest in her work. Finally, we would like to thank Captain Emile Monette, a George Washington University Law student and Government contracts professional, for cite checking and proofreading of the manuscript.

We would also like to dedicate this book to our Government contract clients—today as well as those in the past. These contractors work hard to provide the Government with high-quality goods and services and seek only one thing in return—a fair profit. We hope that those outside as well as inside the Government use this book for its intended purposes—to make sure all those participating in Government contracting know their rights and remedies, and work together to achieve the goals of the United States.

Washington, D.C.　　　　　　　　　　　Richard D. Lieberman
May 2004　　　　　　　　　　　　　　　Karen R. O'Brien

ABOUT THE AUTHORS

Richard D. Lieberman is a partner in the law firm of McCarthy, Sweeney & Harkaway, P.C. He has been directly or indirectly involved in Government contracts for his entire 36-year career and now concentrates exclusively on all aspects of Government contracts law. He served in the Office of the Secretary of Defense, on the staff of the U.S. Senate Appropriations Committee, and in the Office of the Department of Defense Inspector General. Since 1988, he has been in the private practice of law and has concentrated on bid and proposal preparation counseling, bid protests, contract administration, disputes and claims, audits, investigations, and debarment. Mr. Lieberman is the co-author of *Elements of Contract Administration* (2d ed. 2001) and *Elements of Contract Formation* (2000) with Karen R. O'Brien. He received a J.D. from Georgetown University, an M.A. from the University of Wisconsin—Madison, and a B.A. from Cornell University.

Karen R. O'Brien is of counsel in the law firm of McCarthy, Sweeney & Harkaway, P.C. and has over 16 years experience in Government contracting, first in the Army Judge Advocate General's Corp and then as editor of the Nash and Cibinic works. In addition, Ms. O'Brien is co-author on *Competitive Negotiation: The Source Selection Process* (2d ed. 1999) with John Cibinic Jr. and Ralph C. Nash, Jr.; *The Government Contracts Reference Book* (2d ed. 1998) with Ralph C. Nash, Jr. and Steven L. Schooner; and *Elements of Contract Formation* (2000) and *Elements of Contract Administration* (2d ed. 2001) with Richard D. Lieberman. Ms. O'Brien received a B.A. in accounting, magna cum laude, from Niagara University and a J.D., cum laude, from Vermont Law School.

SUMMARY TABLE OF CONTENTS

CONTENTS

Chapter 4
Administration of Government Contracts 105

CHAPTER 1

BASIC PRINCIPLES

The operations of an enterprise as large as the Government of the United States cannot be performed by Government employees alone. Indeed, the work of the Executive Branch, which is principally responsible for the execution and administration of the laws and programs of our Government required the purchase of more than $230 billion of goods and services in fiscal year ("FY") 2002. In FY 2002 the Department of Defense ("DOD") spent $154.4 billion and all civilian agencies combined spent $80.5 billion. Services was the largest category of purchases with $98.8 billion spent in 2002, supplies and equipment were nearly as high with $84.3 billion spent. Finally, while some federal procurement money was spent in every one of the 50 states, the geographic distribution of the money tends to be clustered in nine states (California, Virginia, Texas, Maryland, Florida, New York, Pennsylvania, Georgia, and Arizona) and the District of Columbia. These areas have large concentrations of military and National Aeronautics and Space Administration or Department of Energy installations.

This chapter looks at the basic principles of Government contracting. The first section covers the authority of Government personnel. The second section discusses the statutory and regulatory law governing procurement. The third section alerts readers to the importance of making truthful statements to the Government. The chapter next provides a comparison between Government and commercial contracts and concludes with a discussion of the Freedom of Information Act.

I. AUTHORITY OF GOVERNMENT PERSONNEL

A basic tenet of Government contracting is that the Government is not bound by unauthorized acts of its officers or agents.

A. Actual Authority required

Actual authority is required to bind the Government. This has been a longstanding rule:

1

Whatever the form in which the Government functions, anyone entering into an arrangement with the Government takes the risk of having accurately ascertained that he who purports to act for the Government stays within the bounds of his authority. The scope of this authority may be explicitly defined by Congress or be limited by delegated legislation, properly exercised through the rule-making power. And this is so even though, as here, the agent himself may have been unaware of the limitations upon his authority. *See, e.g., Utah Power & Light Co. v. United States*, 243 U.S. 389, 409 (1917); *United States v. Stewart*, 311 U.S. 60 (1940).[1]

B. Delegation of Authority

Federal Acquisition Regulation ("FAR") 1.601 sets forth the contracting authority, which flows from the head of the agency to contracting officers:

[A]uthority and responsibility to contract for authorized supplies and services are vested in the agency head. The agency head may establish contracting activities and delegate broad authority to manage the agency's contracting functions to heads of such contracting activities. Contracts may be entered into and signed on behalf of the Government only by contracting officers. In some agencies, a relatively small number of high level officials are designated contracting officers solely by virtue of their positions. Contracting officers below the level of a head of a contracting activity shall be selected and appointed under [FAR] 1.603.

1.   Designated Contracting Officers

Contracting officers are appointed in writing on Standard Form 1402, Certificate of Appointment.[2] This form must state any limitations on the scope of authority to be exercised. Information concerning this authority shall be made readily available to the public.[3] Within an agency there are often various tiers of contracting officers—based on dollar limitations. The highest tier is a contracting officer who signed the contract and has full

---

[1] *Federal Crop Ins. Corp. v. Merrill*, 332 U.S. 380 (1947).

[2] This form was formerly called a "warrant," and the person who received it a "warranted contracting officer." The term "warrant" is no longer used in the FAR.

[3] FAR 1.602-1(a).

("plenary") authority. Below that may be a contracting officer with authority to sign contracts and changes up to $500,000 in value. And below that may be a contracting officer with authority to sign contracts and changes up to the simplified acquisition threshold.

2. Functional Contracting Officers

Specific nomenclature is used in the Department of Defense to refer to the different types of contracting officers. Contracting officers that award contracts are known as procuring contracting officers ("PCOs"). Frequently, the PCO's title is shortened to contracting officer ("CO"). Contracting officers that administer contracts are known as administrative contracting officers ("ACOs"). Contracting officers that handle contract terminations are known as terminating contracting officers ("TCOs").

3. Authorized Government Representatives

An authorized Government representative should not be confused with a contracting officer. Authorized representatives generally have a much narrower scope of authority than contracting officers. Of particular note, authorized representatives do not have the authority to sign contracts or contract modifications.

Beginning with the development of a solicitation and continuing throughout contract performance, contracting officers function with the assistance of a team of specialists, including those in audit, law, engineering, transportation, and cost, as well as technical specialists such as inspectors and quality assurance personnel. Frequently, contracting officers will have one or more "contract specialists" working for them, to prepare documents for the contracting officer's signature, research problems, and assist the contracting officer.

C. Alternative Ways to Bind the Government

In many instances, a contractor will have dealings with Government personnel who do not possess full contractual authority—those dealings are not necessarily without legal significance. There are several theories used to bind the Government when the contractor has dealt with personnel possessing less than full authority to bind the Government. Although these are important, contractors should always seek to take direction from a contracting officer. Readers are strongly cautioned that direction from someone other than a contracting officer, who has no express written, delegated authority, is most likely *not* binding on the Government.

1. Implied Authority

Apparent authority will not be sufficient to bind the Government. However, the boards and courts have granted relief on the basis of "implied authority." Implied authority is determined under a reasonable person standard. The Claims Court has stated "a person with no actual authority may not gain actual authority through the court-made rule of implied actual authority."[4] In other words, there must have been *some* authority delegated in order to find implied authority. A good example of where this may occur is in the case of an inspector who has authority to accept or reject the work, but no authority to order changes. In such a case if the inspector orders minor adjustments to the work the Government will likely be bound. The boards and court will generally find implied authority when such authority is considered to be an integral part of the duties assigned to a Government employee.

2. Ratification

Ratification is the adoption of an unauthorized act resulting in the act being given effect as if originally authorized.[5] In Government contracting, an unauthorized act may subsequently be ratified by those with authority to bind the Government. Practioners should use caution; ratification is the *exception*, not the rule. FAR 1.602-3(c) provides that ratification may be exercised only when—

(1) Supplies or services have been provided to and accepted by the Government, or the Government otherwise has obtained or will obtain a benefit resulting from performance of the unauthorized commitment;

(2) The ratifying official has the authority to enter into a contractual commitment;

---

[4] *California Sand & Gravel, Inc. v. United States*, 22 Cl. Ct. 19 (1990), *aff'd*, 937 F.2d 624 (Fed. Cir. 1991).

[5] *Restatement, Second, Agency*, § 82.

(3) The resulting contract would otherwise have been proper if made by an appropriate contracting officer;

(4) The contracting officer reviewing the unauthorized commitment determines the price to be fair and reasonable;

(5) The contracting officer recommends payment and legal counsel concurs in the recommendation, unless agency procedures expressly do not require such concurrence;

(6) Funds are available and were available at the time the unauthorized commitment was made; and

(7) The ratification is in accordance with any other limitations prescribed under agency procedures.

3. *Knowledge Imputed to Authorized Personnel*

The courts and boards have imputed knowledge to contracting officers and other authorized persons when the nature of the relationship between the authorized person and the representative establishes a presumption that the authorized person would be informed. A good example here is in the case of a technical representative.

D. Summary Rules for Authority of Government Personnel

1. Know that only contracting officers who have been granted specific authority may bind the Federal Government only up to the amount of their authority. Contracting officer technical representatives ("COTR"), contracting officer representatives ("COR"), and contract specialists normally have no such authority. Similarly, an ACO has only such authority as the contracting officer delegates to him *in writing*. Most ACOs have no authority to change quantity, price, specifications or delivery schedule.

2. Ascertain the authority that has been delegated to each person that will be involved in the awarded contract.

3. Recognize that although "apparent authority" exists in the commercial sector, only actual, written, delegated authority exists in Government contracting.

II. STATUTORY AND REGULATORY LAW

A. Statutes Governing Procurement

There are two major statutes covering most Government procurement—
the Armed Services Procurement Act and the Federal Property and Administrative Services Act. In addition, there are numerous statutes that have an
impact on the procurement process. A brief description of these and other
important procurement statutes follows:

- **Armed Services Procurement Act ("ASPA")**[6] —This statute
  governs the procurement procedures followed by the DOD, the
  National Aeronautics and Space Administration ("NASA"), and
  the Coast Guard. It was enacted in 1947 and has been amended
  numerous times.

- **Federal Property and Administrative Services Act
  ("FPASA")**[7] —This statute contains policies and procedures
  for the procurement of supplies and services, including construction, by almost all federal executive agencies except DOD,
  NASA and the Coast Guard. The FPASA was enacted in 1949
  and, like the ASPA, has been amended numerous times.

- **Competition in Contracting Act ("CICA") of 1984**[8] —This
  statute amended the two basic procurement statutes (ASPA and
  FPASA) to enhance competition. This statute also granted
  statutory authorization for the General Accounting Office's protest function. CICA introduced the phrase "full and open competition," replaced the label "formal advertising" with "sealed
  bidding," and placed competitive negotiation on par with sealed
  bidding as a method that provides for full and open competition.

---

[6] 10 U.S.C. § 2302 *et seq.*

[7] 41 U.S.C. § 251 *et seq.*

[8] 41 U.S.C. § 251 *et seq.*; 10 U.S.C. § 2304 *et seq.*

- **Federal Acquisition Streamlining Act ("FASA") of 1994**[9] — This statute substantially revised federal procurement law. The Act encourages the acquisition of commercial items, raised the threshold for simplified acquisition procedures to $100,000, promotes electronic commerce, and achieves greater efficiency and uniformity among the agencies in their procurement practices.

- **Clinger-Cohen Act of 1996 (also known as the "Federal Acquisition Reform Act" ("FARA"))**[10] —This statute was enacted in 1996 as part of the Fiscal Year 1996 Defense Authorization Act. The Act provides for Government-wide acquisition reform, including the repeal of the Brooks Act, coverage on information technology ("IT") procurement, a shortening of the time permitted for the General Accounting Office to issue bid protest decisions, a revision of the Procurement Integrity Act, and the elimination of certain regulatory certification requirements.

B. Department of Homeland Security

The Department of Homeland Security ("DHS") was created in June 2002 and formally began operations in March 2003. DHS is the third largest federal agency (after Defense and Veterans Affairs). DHS has a budget of approximately $40 billion, of which $28 billion is for contracts and grants. DHS is to generally follow existing, Government-wide procurement laws, but also has broad authority to deviate from those rules if they would "impair" the agency's missions or operations. The Homeland Security Act of 2002, Public Law No. 107-296, provides procurement flexibility provisions to DHS as follows: (1) treating any item or service to be acquired as a "commercial item" for purpose of federal procurement laws; (2) increasing the threshold for simplified acquisition procedures from $5 million to $7.5 million; (3) increasing the simplified acquisition threshold from $125,000 to $175,000; and (4) increasing the micro-purchase threshold from $2,500 to $5,000.[11] Strict approval and reporting obligations are to be followed if these

---

[9] Pub. L. No. 103-355.

[10] Pub. L. No. 104-106.

[11] See subsequent chapters for a discussion of these contract types.

options are used. DHS also possesses special authority to use "other transactions" (i.e., not contracts or grants) to carry out prototype and research and development projects. This authority is similar to the authority in the DOD for "other transactions."

As part of the Homeland Security Act, Congress enacted the Support Anti-Terrorism by Fostering Effective Technologies Act of 2002 ("SAFETY Act")[12] to provide "risk management" and "litigation management" protections for sellers of qualified anti-terrorism technologies and others in the supply and distribution chain. The aim of the Act is to encourage the development and deployment of anti-terrorism technologies that will substantially enhance the protection of the nation. Specifically, the SAFETY Act creates certain liability limitations for "claims arising out of, relating to, or resulting from an act of terrorism" where qualified anti-terrorism technologies have been deployed.

C. Federal Acquisition Regulatory System

Most Federal Government contracts are subject to the Federal Acquisition Regulation ("FAR"),[13] and almost all of those contracts are also subject to the requirements in various agency supplements to the FAR.[14] See **Figure 1-1**. The FAR and its supplements are known as the "FAR system."[15] It is therefore essential that a prospective contractor determine the applicable regulations, directives, and instructions *prior* to submitting a bid or proposal for the contract, and then ensure that it maintains a current and complete set

---

[12] Pub. L. No. 107-296, Nov. 25, 2002.

[13] 48 C.F.R. Title I.

[14] FAR 1.301(a)(1) authorizes agencies to issue "agency acquisition regulations that implement or supplement the FAR, and incorporate . . . agency policies, procedures, contract clauses, solicitation provisions, and forms" that govern the contract. In addition, FAR 1.301(a)(2) permits agencies to issue "internal agency guidance." The most recently issued FAR Supplement is the Department of Homeland Security Acquisition Regulation ("HSAR"), Part 30 of Title 48, Code of Federal Regulations, 68 Fed. Reg. 67868 (Dec. 4, 2003). See http://www.dhs.gov/dhspublic/.

[15] The FAR is available on the Internet at www.arnet.gov. It is also part of the CCH Government Contracts Research Library at www.business.cch.com.

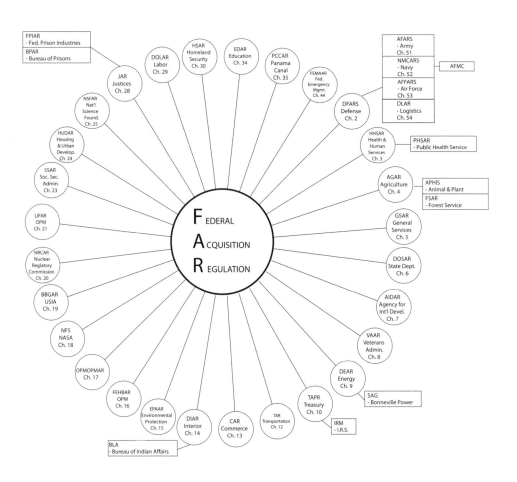

Figure 1-1

throughout the term of the awarded contract. For example, a contract issued by an Army installation such as Fort Hood would be subject to the FAR, the

Department of Defense FAR Supplement ("DFARS"),[16] the Army Federal Acquisition Regulation Supplement ("AFARS"),[17] any Army command directive or instruction that applies to Fort Hood, and perhaps even some local Fort Hood instruction or regulation. Although the FAR and the agency supplements are readily available on the Internet, in libraries, from the Government Printing Office, and from commercial services (including searchable copies on CD-ROM disks), the local directives or instructions are usually available only from the agency.

Prior to preparing a bid or proposal, every prospective contractor should read or be familiar with the full text of all clauses that will be included in the contract. If the contract references or is subject to any unpublished agency regulations, a copy of those regulations should be requested from the contracting officer and kept current throughout the life of the contract. Virtually every contract contains 75 or more standard FAR, DFARS, or agency clauses that are either included in full text in the solicitation or merely referenced in the solicitation and "incorporated by reference."[18] The contractor will be required to comply with all of them. A prospective contractor must never give only a cursory reading to the solicitation, believing that the statement of work is the most important part of the contract while the rest is "boilerplate." That approach is both unwise and potentially very dangerous. The "boilerplate" includes many clauses that impose significant obligations and requirements on the contractor. For example, FAR 52.222-4, Contract Work Hours and Safety Standards Act— Overtime Compensation; FAR 52.222-6, Davis-Bacon Act; and FAR 52.222-41, Service Contract Act of 1965, as amended, all require the contractor to pay certain minimum wages, fringe benefits, and overtime amounts to employees. A bid or proposal must include amounts to cover these wages or it will either be deemed unrealistic (if it is a cost-reimbursement contract) or could cause a company serious financial loss if the contract is fixed price.

---

[16] 48 C.F.R. Chapter 2.

[17] 48 C.F.R. Chapter 51.

[18] Incorporation by reference is a technique whereby the number of the clause and its heading are listed, but the text of the clause is not. This listing provides the same legal force and effect as if the clause were printed in full text. *See* FAR 52.252-2, Clauses Incorporated by Reference.

1. How FAR Clauses are Numbered

FAR Subpart 52.2 contains all FAR provisions and clauses, and is arranged by subject matter, in the same order as, and keyed to, the first 51 parts of the FAR. All FAR clauses begin with "52.2." The next two digits of the provision or clause number correspond to the number of the FAR subject part in which the provision or clause is prescribed. When there are multiple clauses, the number will be followed by "-1," "-2," etc.

A typical example is as follows: FAR 52.243-1 is the clause for "Changes-Fixed Price." The first two digits in the clause (52.2) are the same for all FAR clauses. The next two digits (43) are taken from FAR Part 43— the part that prescribes this clause. FAR Part 43 is titled "Contract Modifications," and modifications is another word for changes. FAR 43.205(a)(1) states that the "contracting officer shall insert the clause at 52.243-1, Changes-Fixed Price, in solicitations and contracts when a fixed-price contract for supplies is contemplated." The introduction to FAR 52.243-1 states "as prescribed in [FAR] 43.205(a)(1), insert the following clause."

2. Which Version of the FAR Clause Is Applicable

The general rule is that the FAR clause in effect at the time of execution of the contract (and presumably included in the solicitation and contract) applies to that contract. The clause in the contract at the time of award governs the contractor's rights and obligations, and the Government may not change these clauses without the contactor's agreement through a modification of the contract.

Many times, when major changes are made to numerous FAR clauses, contracting officers will make wholesale modifications to contracts. They will delete old, out-of-date clauses, and substitute the new FAR clauses. If a modification is made to a contractor's contract, the contractor will be bound by the new clause. As with any modification, it requires the contractor's concurrence. Contractors should examine any new clause proferred by the contracting officer. Contractors may reject it outright or demand other changes, including a price increase. If a contractor is unwilling to accept the new clause, the Government may issue a change order incorporating the new clause. However, in such a case, the contractor is permitted to obtain an equitable adjustment in price or delivery schedule depending on the impact of the change.

D. Summary Rules for Statutory and Regulatory Laws

1. Know and understand the basic statutes and regulations that control Government procurement. In particular become fully acquainted with the FAR system.

2. Understand the importance of incorporation by reference, since many clauses are included in contracts in that manner.

3. Become familiar with all clauses in a solicitation before submitting an offer, and with all clauses in the contract before beginning contract performance.

4. Understand how the FAR is numbered.

5. Know which version of a FAR clause applies to your contract.

III.   HONESTY AND DISCLOSURE OF FACTS

In all dealings with the Government, including written certifications, telephone calls, and meetings with contract officials, contractors must provide only truthful statements. Any deception or intentional misdealings with federal officials (contractual or otherwise) could have serious consequences. When an investigation occurs and problems are found, the most common charges involve criminal false statements, criminal and civil false claims, mail and wire fraud, and obstruction of justice.

A. Criminal and Civil Statutes

The following is a list of some of the statutes most frequently used in prosecuting Government contractors:

- **Criminal False Statements**[19]—Prohibiting anyone from knowingly and willfully falsifying, concealing, or covering up a material fact by any trick, scheme, or device, or making or using any false, fictitious, or fraudulent statement, representation, writing or document, in any matter within the jurisdiction of any U.S. Government

---

[19] 18 U.S.C. § 1001.

agency. Penalties: imprisonment up to five years and a fine up to $250,000 for each false statement.[20]

- **Criminal False Claims**[21]—Prohibiting anyone from making or presenting to the U.S. Government any claim against the United States, knowing such claim to be false, fictitious, or fraudulent. Proof beyond a reasonable doubt is required. Penalties: imprisonment up to five years and a fine up to $250,000 for each false claim.

- **Civil False Claims**[22]—Prohibiting anyone from knowingly presenting to the U.S. Government a false or fraudulent claim for payment. Proof by a preponderance of the evidence is required—a lesser standard than the proof beyond a reasonable doubt needed to prove a criminal false claim. Penalties: for each false claim, a fine of between $5,000 and $10,000 plus three times the amount of loss sustained by the Government. Civil false claim actions often follow a criminal false statement or false claims conviction and thereby substantially increase the penalties.

- **Mail and Wire Fraud**[23]—Prohibiting anyone from using the mail or the wires, radio, or TV to execute a scheme or artifice to defraud or to obtain money or property by means of false or fraudulent pretenses. Penalties: imprisonment up to five years and a fine of up to $250,000 for each fraudulent use of the mail or wires.

- **Conspiracy**[24]—Prohibiting two or more persons from conspiring either to commit any offense against the United States or to defraud the United States in any manner, where one person takes at least one overt act in furtherance of the conspiracy. Penalties: imprisonment up to five years and a fine of up to $250,000.

---

[20] Sentence of fine, 18 U.S.C. § 3571.

[21] 18 U.S.C. § 287.

[22] 31 U.S.C. § 3729.

[23] 18 U.S.C. § 1341 and § 1343.

[24] 18 U.S.C. § 371.

- **Obstruction**[25]—Obstructing or endeavoring to obstruct or impede the due administration of justice or administration of federal law. Penalties: imprisonment up to 10 years and a fine of up to $250,000.

Investigators and prosecutors often charge violations of several different laws for any given scheme perpetrated by a Government contractor. For example, if two persons conspire to submit a false progress payment, and the voucher for the payment is sent through the mails, the Government could charge mail fraud, a criminal false statement or a false claim, and conspiracy. Once there is a criminal conviction, the Government could seek substantial damages by charging a civil false claim. In addition, conviction on any of these offenses will likely lead to contractor debarment (exclusion from contract award) for three or more years.[26]

B. Case Illustrations

Many former Government contractors and officials are today in jail, on probation, or paying substantial fines for failing to deal honestly with the Government. The following is a list of some cases that illustrate the potential severity of conviction, divided between fraud during formation and fraud in performance:

Formation of contracts

- *United States v. Anderson*[27] —An 8(a)[28] contractor, a minority business specialist for the Small Business Administration ("SBA"), and the principal of a large construction company entered into a conspiracy to defraud the Government. The 8(a) contractor was the owner of Kathy's Kranes, a woman-owned business. With the SBA business specialist's help she was able to obtain noncompetitive contracts at the SBA by submitting

---

[25] 18 U.S.C. § 1503 and § 1505.

[26] FAR 9.405 and 9.406-2.

[27] 879 F.2d 369 (8th Cir. 1989), *cert. denied*, 493 U.S. 982 (1989).

[28] This refers to Section 8(a) of the Small Business Investment Act of 1958, codified at 15 U.S.C. § 637(a), the Government's program to set-aside contracts for small disadvantaged contractors that meet certain requirements. *See also* FAR Subpart 19.8, 13 C.F.R. Part 124, and Chapter 3 of this book.

forms and certifications that did not disclose her affiliation with the large construction company, a non-8(a) participant. The contractor and the large construction company had an agreement that the construction company would give the 8(a) the needed equipment and personnel to do the projects in return for a percentage of the profits. All the individuals were convicted of knowingly and willfully making false statements and of conspiracy to defraud the United States by impeding, impairing, obstructing, and defeating the administration of the 8(a) program.

- *United States v. Merklinger*[29] —Alex G. Merklinger, bidding on DOD construction contracts, signed Affidavits of Individual Surety forms that contained fraudulent asset figures and signed letters of credit for $2 million to a Government construction officer for the purpose of qualifying as a surety on a Government-funded project even though he knew he could not pay. He was convicted of mail fraud, wire fraud, and falsely making guarantees pertaining to a bond. He was sentenced to 37 months on each charge to run concurrently, three years of supervised release, and a $6,000 fine.

- *United States v. Rogers*[30] —Individual and corporate defendants were convicted of mail fraud and of making false statements to the U.S. Army Corps of Engineers. Members of the river construction industry of the Mississippi River and its major tributaries between 1964–78 engaged in a bid-rigging scheme to arrange bids in order to ensure that a contractor, which had been agreed to by the river contractors, would receive the contract award. They did this by agreeing on the prices (or "no bids") to be submitted by the bidders. In addition, each bidder certified that the prices in the bid had been arrived at independently, without consultation, communication or agreement with other bidders for the purpose of restrictive competition. These certifications were false statements under 18 U.S.C. § 1001.

---

[29] 16 F.3d 670 (6th Cir. 1994).

[30] 624 F.2d 1303 (5th Cir. 1980).

- *United States v. Puente*[31] —Roberto Puente, Jr. and his father were each convicted of making a false statement to the U.S. Department of Housing and Urban Development ("HUD"), a violation of 18 U.S.C. § 1001. HUD required that a "Prior Participation Certification" form be submitted with their bid on renovation of a housing project. Both had certified on the HUD certification form that they had never been convicted of a felony, although each had a previous felony conviction.

- *United States v. Davis*[32]—Carolyn Ann Davis pled guilty to making false statements in violation of 18 U.S.C. § 1001 for falsely representing in her bid on a hangar-painting contract submitted to the U.S. Air Force that neither her firm nor any of its principals (of which she was the only one) was presently debarred or had been convicted within the prior three years of making false statements. In fact, Ms. Davis had been debarred on account of an October 1989 conviction of making false statements. Ms. Davis used her maiden name, Carolyn Smith, in the August 1991 bid in order to avoid detection.

Administration of contracts

- *United States v. Leo*[33]

  General Electric, doing business as Management & Technical Services Inc. ("MATSCO"), contracted with the Army for production of mobile battlefield computer systems housed in trailers. Gerald Leo, responsible for purchasing materials, and James Badolato, subcontract manager, conspired to defraud the Army of millions of dollars to advance their standing in the company. They made fraudulent statements as to subcontractor costs in negotiations, suggested that subcontractors pad their quotes for unanticipated costs, and altered purchase orders. MATSCO was convicted on four counts of mail fraud and 282 counts of False Claim Act violations and paid a $10 million criminal fine. (General Electric paid

---

[31] 982 F.2d 156 (5th Cir. 1993).

[32] 14 F.3d 605 (7th Cir. 1993). The case deals with application of the Federal Sentencing Guidelines, but the underlying conviction is fully explained.

[33] 941 F.2d 181 (3d Cir. 1991).

$8.3 million in civil damages, $11.7 million to resolve other civil damages, and agreed not to appeal.) Leo was convicted on four counts of mail fraud, sentenced to 10 months' imprisonment, and ordered to pay $15,000 for his conviction on false statements. Badolato received five months' imprisonment for obstruction of an agency investigation and paid a $10,000 fine for false statements.

- ***United States. v. Langer***[34]

  Central Manufacturing was awarded an SBA contract with the Air Force for 13 tank-type potable water distributor semitrailers. Central subcontracted with Fred Langer for engineering services and supervision of assembly of first article testing ("FAT"). Langer did not build the tanks and trailers to specifications, falsified reports on FAT results, and doubled the price of materials on invoices. He was convicted of mail fraud and of fraudulently misrepresenting that the tanks and trailers conformed to specifications. Langer was sentenced to two years' imprisonment, four years' probation, fined $10,000, and ordered to pay $251,000 restitution for the false statements.

- ***United States v. Castner***[35]

  Systems Engineering, Inc. ("SEI"), had a prime contract with the Navy to repair, refurbish, and maintain computer tape drive systems using only parts that met Miltrope Corp's specifications and to purchase them only from the Navy Supply System, Miltrope, or a Miltrope-authorized company. Because of problems in securing these parts, two principals of SEI created a company called Gali Resources, Inc. ("GRI"), to be an affiliate of SEI in order to obtain reverse-engineered Miltrope parts from unapproved sources. They obtained or assembled these parts at low cost and then sold them to SEI at a substantial price increase. SEI then charged the Navy the price they paid GRI plus a 9 percent inventory support charge and a 5 percent material handling cost. They were convicted of fraud against the United States and of mail fraud. One principal received a 27-month imprisonment and was ordered to pay a $6,000 fine, a $1,300 special assessment, and $50,000 in retribution. The other

---

[34] 962 F.2d 592 (7th Cir. 1992).

[35] 50 F.3d 1267 (4th Cir. 1995).

principal received 21-month imprisonment and was ordered to pay a $5,000 fine, a $1,300 special assessment, and $37,500 in retribution.

- *United States v. Philips Electronics North America Corporation*[36]

    Philips falsified test data, destroyed data on test failures, destroyed noncompliant resistors, and submitted false and fraudulent documents to the Defense Supply Center in order to remain on the DOD qualified products list. Philips was convicted of conspiracy to make false representations to the DOD, 17 counts of falsification of test data, and destruction of DOD documents. The company received the maximum fine of $9 million and was ordered to set aside another $5 million for customer claims and to notify customers of its conviction.

C. Summary Rules for Honesty and Disclosure of Facts

1. Be scrupulously honest and accurate in all dealings with the Government, written or oral.

2. Understand the criminal and civil statutes that affect Government contracts.

3. Make only accurate statements to the Government. Statements include those made orally or in writing.

IV. GOVERNMENT AND COMMERCIAL CONTRACTS COMPARED

Because most readers are familiar with the way that commercial contracts are formed and executed, it is helpful to understand the similarities and differences between commercial and Government contracts. All contracts, whether Government or commercial, represent an agreement between two or more parties that creates a mutual obligation to do or not to do a particular thing. In general, all contracts are formed through the issuance of an offer to

---

[36] Unpublished decision (N.D. TX 1995).

perform or not perform something, the acceptance of the offer by the other party, and the inclusion of consideration (usually the payment of money or some detriment or forbearance by one of the parties). The principal differences between Government and commercial contracts are in the statutory and regulatory framework, the types of contracts used, the authority of agents who form the contracts, and the special clauses or requirements contained in most Government contracts. These differences are discussed below and summarized in **Figure 1-2**.

Figure 1-2: Government vs. Commercial Contracting

Aspect	Commercial Contracting	Government Contracting
Statutory and Regulatory framework	UCC, common law	USC Titles 10, 40, 41, FAR, DFARS, others UCC
Type of contract	Mostly firm-fixed-price, oral	Firm-fixed-price, cost-reimbursement, no oral
Competition Requirements	No such requirement	Full and open
Authority of agents	Apparent authority	Only actual, written authority
Audits	Rare	Fact of life
Socioeconomic programs	Not required	Mandatory
Protests, claims, and disputes	None	Normal and routine
Changes clause	Mutual agreement	Government change order
Termination for Convenience clause	No such clause	Required

A. Statutory and Regulatory Framework

Government contracts are subject to an extensive statutory framework contained in title 10 (Armed Forces) and title 41 (Public Contracts and Property Management) of the United States Code, and an extensive regulatory framework in the FAR as well as other applicable regulations. Commercial contracts for goods are subject to a much less complex framework, namely, Article 2 of the Uniform Commercial Code ("UCC"), which governs sales of goods, has been adopted by 49 of the states and the District of Columbia (Louisiana has not adopted Article 2 of the UCC). The UCC is relatively simple and has been in effect for almost 50 years. Included within the statutory and regulatory framework for Government contracts is a requirement for *full and open competition*, a term of art discussed later. No such competition requirement exists for commercial contracts. The statutory and regulatory framework provides for Government *audits* of federal contractors, a fact of life that accompanies doing business with the Government, but something which is generally not used (i.e., one contractor auditing another contractor) in the commercial contracting world. In addition, statutes require that the Government support certain *socioeconomic programs*, and provide such things as set-asides for small businesses only, or noncompetitive awards to socially and economically disadvantaged businesses. Few commercial contracts require such affirmative socioeconomic programs. Finally, the statutory framework provides for an impartial and extensive process for submitting *protests* to the Government concerning violation of laws or regulations in the formation of Government contracts. In the commercial world, losing offerors have virtually no basis upon which to question the selection of a contractor that has been made by another private entity.

B. Authority of Agents

As discussed previously, in the Federal Government, contracts may be entered into, signed and modified on behalf of the Government *only* by contracting officers who have been granted specific authority in writing to do so. This written delegation to the contracting officer is frequently known as a "warrant," and contracting officers are often referred to as "warranted contracting officers" because they have legal authority to bind the Government *up to the amount of their warrant* (written delegation from the agency head). In Government contracting, the only type of authority that is permitted is the *express authority* described above. In commercial contracting, agents (such as a purchasing agent, a corporate vice president, or any person acting on behalf of a company) may have either express or *apparent authority*, and the state laws will consider that binding contracts have been formed or modified by those with apparent authority. Apparent authority is the power which a third party can reasonably assume that an agent possesses, e.g., a purchasing agent may bind his company to pay for the purchases he makes on the company's behalf, a production manager may bind his company to pay for the purchases he makes for production. The courts will enforce contracts made by agents with apparent authority in the private sector,[37] but no such apparent authority will bind the Government in its contracts.

C. Types of Contracts

The Federal Government uses two principal types of contracts: *firm-fixed-price* and *cost-reimbursement*. A firm-fixed-price contract is just that—the price is agreed upon in advance and the contractor must perform for that price. More than 60 percent of the dollar amounts awarded by the Federal Government are in firm-fixed-price contracts. It is very similar to standard home repair or home improvement contracts used by most consumers. A cost-reimbursement contract permits the contractor to obtain payment from the Government for all of the contractor's reasonable, allowable and allocable costs incurred in performing the contract. Cost-reimbursement contracts are generally used where there is high risk (such as developing a new aircraft, or placing a person on the moon), and that risk is in the national interest and should properly be borne by the Government, not the contractor. Almost all commercial contracts, including subcontracts under many different Government contracts, are *fixed price*. That is because the nature of the item or work (including the specifications) tends to be known in advance, and there are few large scale development programs undertaken by private contractors. The fixed-price contract for Government work or products is very similar to the fixed-price commercial contract.

---

[37] "A principal is bound by the acts of an agent performed with apparent authority where the third person acted upon reliance of apparent authority held out by the principal." *Moncrief v. Wilston Basin Intersate Pipeline Co.*, 880 F. Supp. 1495, 1512 (D. Wyo. 1995), *aff'd in part, rev'd in part & remanded by* 174 F.3d 1150 (10th cir. 1999), *citing Kure v. Chevrolet Motor Div.*, 581 P.2d 603, 609 (Wyo. 1978). *See also Restatement (Second) of Agency* § 8 (1958).

D. Changes and Termination for Convenience Clauses

Government contracts contain two unique clauses *not* found in commercial contracts: the Changes clause and the Termination for the Convenience of the Government clause. In commercial contracts, any change (such as the upgrading of materials, increase in size of a room, or change in specifications) requires the *mutual agreement of both parties*. The contractor need not undertake any change until it has obtained agreement on how the contract will be changed, including a price change if necessary. A Government contract incorporates a unique Changes clause,[38] which permits the Government to unilaterally *order* the contractor to make changes within the scope of the contract, without obtaining the contractor's agreement. The contractor is required to make the change, but may seek an equitable adjustment (usually an increase) in price or delivery time as a result of the change. Probably the most unique clause in a Government contract is the Termination for the Convenience of the Government ("T/C") clause, which permits the Government to terminate the contract in whole or in part if a termination is in the Government's interest.[39] No similar clause exists in commercial contracts. The purpose of the T/C clause is to permit the Government to stop work in a timely manner on such things as military supplies, vehicles, or aircraft that are no longer needed when a war ends, for example, or to terminate contracts when the Congress refuses to continue funding for the projects. Upon receipt of a T/C, the contractor must stop work, terminate subcontracts, and efficiently close out the contract. The contractor is entitled to submit a termination proposal and to be paid by the Government its costs and profit *up to the date of termination*. The concept underlying a T/C is that the Government needs to stop the contract and it will be stopped, but the contractor will not be harmed, because the Government will pay the contractor for all costs incurred that were necessary to close out the contract efficiently.[40]

---

[38] *See, e.g.*, FAR 52.243-1 (Changes—Fixed Price).

[39] *See, e.g.*, FAR 52.249-2 (Termination for the Convenience of the Government—Fixed-Price).

[40] The most unusual aspect of the T/C and Changes clauses is that the Government *does not* require that similar clauses be included in subcontracts awarded by prime Government contractors. If the prime contractor fails to include them, it may be impossible to stop the subcontractor's work or deliveries

E. Summary Rules for Government and Commercial Contracts Compared

1. Know and understand the basic statutes and regulations that control Government procurement. In particular become fully acquainted with the FAR system.

2. Recognize that while the commercial sector primarily uses fixed-price type contracts, the Government uses both fixed price and cost-reimbursement contracts.

3. Understand that two unique aspects of Government contracting are the Changes and the Termination for Convenience clauses. The Changes clause permits the Government to order changes within the scope of the contract, even without the concurrence of the contractor. The Termination for Convenience clause permits the Government to terminate the contract at any time if it is in the Government's best interest.

4. Both the changes and Termination for Convenience clauses should be included by a prime contractor in any subcontract it awards.

V. FREEDOM OF INFORMATION ACT

The Freedom of Information Act ("FOIA")[41] provides a means by which any person may gain access to information in the Government's possession. The Act provides that "each agency, upon any request for records which (A) reasonably describes such records, and (B) is made in accordance with published rules stating the time, place, fees (if any), and procedures to be followed, shall make the records promptly available to any person." The Act is available to anyone—including persons not party to a controversy. The Act *requires* that requested records be furnished unless one of nine statutory exemptions applies.[42] The FOIA is especially useful for obtaining copies of

---

in the case of a T/C, or it may be impossible to change the specifications where the Government orders a change. This would mean great cost to the prime contractor. As explained later in this book, it is essential that every prime contractor include both of these clauses in every subcontract it awards.

[41] 5 U.S.C. § 552.

[42] 5 U.S.C. § 552(b).

a competitor's contract, or a previously awarded contract that has a similar specification or statement of work to one in which you are interested. Even if some portion of the requested contract is "redacted" (i.e., deleted), it still may prove very helpful.

A. Agency Record

When requesting information under FOIA, it is important to properly formulate the request. The request must be for agency records. The term "agency records" includes "products of data compilation, such as all books, papers, maps, and photographs, machine readable materials, inclusive of those in electronic form or format, or other documentary materials, regardless of physical form or characteristics, made or received by an agency."[43] Records in electronic format are agency records which must be made available in that format if so requested. The other important thing to note is that for something to be an agency record, it must be in both the possession and control of the agency.

B. Exemptions

As stated above, there are nine exemptions to FOIA. These exemptions are as follows:

(1) specially authorized under criteria established by an Executive order to be kept secret in the interest of national defense or foreign policy;

(2) related solely to the internal personnel rules and practices of any agency;

(3) specifically exempted from disclosure by statute;

(4) trade secrets and commercial or final information obtained from a person or privileged or confidential;

---

[43] DOD Freedom of Information Act Program Regulation 5400.7-R, 62 Fed. Reg. 35351, July 1, 1997.

(5) inter-agency or intra-agency memorandums or letters which would not be available by law to a party other than an agency in litigation with the agency;

(6) personnel and medical files and similar files the disclosure of which would constitute a clearly unwarranted invasion of personal privacy;

(7) records or information compiled for law enforcement purposes;

(8) contained in or related to examination, operating, or condition reports prepared by, on behalf of, or for the use of an agency responsible for the regulation or supervision of financial institutions; and

(9) geological or geophysical information and data, including maps, concerning wells.

C. Preparing a FOIA Request

Any request for information under FOIA must be directed in writing to the FOIA officer as prescribed in the agency's FOIA regulations, which can be found in the Code of Federal Regulations and are frequently set forth in the agency's Internet site. Usually the request should be made to the person that has possession and control of the documents. The request should clearly set forth each and every document that the party wishes to obtain. General statements will not suffice. The letter should also state that the party agrees to pay any copying fees. It is also good to state the following in any request: "5 U.S.C. § 552(a)(6)(A)(i) requires that your agency determine within 20 working days after receipt of this request whether the agency will comply and immediately notify the undersigned of the agency's determination, the reasons therefore and appeal rights in the event of an adverse determination." The primary objective of this language is to let the agency know that you understand your FOIA rights. If an agency fails to comply with a request within 20 days or in the event of an adverse determination, a party may appeal.

D. Summary Rules for Freedom of Information Act

1. Always check the specific agency's FOIA regulations prior to submitting a request.

2. Be specific and identify the agency record(s) sought. Most FOIA requests must be by letter, although some agencies permit electronic (email) requests.

3. Follow up every request to ensure that the agency responds in a timely manner.

CHAPTER 2

FORMATION OF GOVERNMENT CONTRACTS

This chapter covers the formation of contracts—meaning the submission of bids or proposals and the Government selection of a contractor for award. It stresses the differing requirements for competition in different types of contracting, ranging from "full and open competition" through "competition to the maximum extent practicable" to no competition (e.g. "sole source buy"). The chapter also explains the types of contracts used in Government contracting, and the two principal methods by which contracts are formed (negotiated procurement and sealed bidding).

I. PROPER BUSINESS PRACTICES

Many business practices that are acceptable in private commercial contracting are outlawed in Federal Government contracting. Every contractor must understand the laws and regulations concerning improper business practices and various conflicts of interest.

A. Standards of Conduct

The Government is required to conduct its business in a manner above reproach, with complete impartiality and with preferential treatment for none.[44] Standards of conduct for Government employees generally prohibit the giving of gifts of anything of value by anyone, including contractors, to Government personnel, and the acceptance of such gifts.[45] The right of a contractor to proceed with a contract may be terminated if a contractor gives a gratuity to an officer, employee or official of the United States if such a gratuity is intended to obtain a contract or favorable treatment under a contract.[46]

---

[44] FAR 3.101-1.

[45] 5 C.F.R. Parts 2635 and 2636.

[46] FAR 52.203-3.

B. Independent Pricing

The prices in contractor's bids or proposals submitted to the Government must be arrived at independently without any consultation, communication or agreement with any other offeror or competitor. Offerors must certify to the independence of their pricing when submitting a bid or offer.[47] The regulations state if contracting personnel detect pricing that appears to eliminate competition or restrain trade, such as collusive bidding, follow-the-leader pricing, rotated low bids, collusive price estimating systems or sharing of the business, these personnel must report any evidence to the Attorney General as well as the office responsible for suspension and debarment of contractors.[48]

C. Procurement Integrity

The Procurement Integrity Act, as amended by the Clinger-Cohen Act of 1996,[49] prohibits a "person" from knowingly obtaining "contractor bid or proposal information" or "source selection information" before the award of the "Federal agency procurement" to which the information relates.[50] The Act applies only to a "federal agency procurement."

"Contractor proposal information" is any of the information submitted to a federal agency as part of or in connection with a bid or proposal to enter into a federal agency procurement contract. This includes cost or pricing data, labor rates, indirect costs, proprietary information or data marked by the contractor as "contractor bid or proposal information" in accordance with applicable law or regulation.[51]

The term "source selection information" includes bid prices, proposed costs or prices, source selection plans, cost and technical evaluations of proposals and associated rankings and reports. This prohibition is very

---

[47] FAR 52.203-2.

[48] FAR 3.301(b).

[49] Pub. L. No. 104-106.

[50] 41 U.S.C. § 423(b).

[51] 41 U.S.C. § 423(f).

broad. It applies to *any contractor, other business entity, or individual that obtains information*—even if that person is not involved in the procurement.

Violations of the Procurement Integrity Act are punishable by both criminal penalties and civil fines. Until 1994, contractors were required to certify in every offer that they had not violated the Procurement Integrity Act. Although this certification was eliminated by The Federal Acquisition Streamlining Act ("FASA"), offerors must still comply with the underlying law.

D. Prohibition Against Contingent Fees that Lead to Improper Influence

Contractors must include a warranty or "covenant" against the use of contingent fees where such fees lead to attempted or actual exercise of improper influence.[52]

E. Subcontractor Kickbacks

A kickback is any money, fee, credit, gift, or other thing of value which is provided directly or indirectly to any prime contractor, employee of a prime contractor, subcontractor or subcontractor employee for the purpose of improperly obtaining or rewarding favorable treatment in connection with a prime or subcontract.[53] The Anti-Kickback Act of 1986[54] prohibits any person from providing, attempting or offering to provide any kickback, or soliciting such a kickback. It also prohibits any person from including, directly or directly, the amount of any kickback in the contract price (prime or subcontractor) charged to the Federal Government. Civil and criminal penalties may be imposed for violations. An anti-kickback clause is required in all federal contracts exceeding the simplified acquisition threshold, other than those for commercial items.[55]

---

[52] 10 U.S.C. §2306(b) and 41 U.S.C. § 254(a); FAR 3.402, FAR 52.203-5.

[53] FAR 3.502-1.

[54] 41 U.S.C. §§51-58.

[55] FAR 3.502-3, FAR 52.203-7.

F. Summary Rules for Proper Business Practices

1.   Become familiar with the rules and statutes covering proper business practices.

2.   Do not give gifts or gratuities to agency officials.

3.   Do not engage in anti-competitive behavior, such as collusive bidding.

4.   Comply with the procurement integrity rules, the prohibition against contingent fees, and the Anti-Kickback Act.

II. COMPETITION AND METHODS OF CONTRACTING

The requirement for competition and the selection of the contracting technique are key concepts in Government contracting. Contractors must understand these concepts if they are going to compete effectively for a Government contract.

A. Competition Requirement in Government Procurement

Competition is a major goal in Federal Government contracting. It is believed that adequate competition ensures that the Government will receive prices that are fair and reasonable. If an offeror knows that it has competition in a procurement, then it is more likely to offer a price that is fair and reasonable and in line with its actual costs (along with a reasonable profit) because it understands that if it does not another offeror will.

The Competition in Contracting Act ("CICA") of 1984 specifically requires "full and open competition" to be attained by executive agencies in the conduct of sealed bid or competitive negotiation except as specifically permitted by statute. "Full and open competition" basically means that all responsible sources are permitted to compete for a contract. There are also five other very specialized "competitive procedures" which are included in the definition of full and open competition.[56] Realizing that in some in-

---

[56] The five procedures are: (1) procurement of architectural or engineering services, (2) the competitive selection for award of basic research proposals,

stances receiving an inordinately large number of proposals in negotiated procurements can bog down the process, Congress, in 1996, added a new provision to the statutes, which mandates that the requirement to obtain full and open competition be "implemented in a manner that is consistent with the need to efficiently fulfill the Government's requirements."[57] In an effort to obtain efficiency, contracting officers can limit the number of proposals in the competitive range "to the greatest number that will permit an efficient competition among the offerors rated most highly."[58] This is explained in Section V of this chapter.

There are only seven specific procurement situations where full and open competition is *not* required. These are:

1. **Only one responsible source**[59] —This exception is intended to permit a sole source procurement. An agency determination that a prospective contractor is the only source capable of meeting the agency's needs is subject to close scrutiny. The availability of only one source must be demonstrated convincingly.[60]

- A sole source procurement may be justified if the *items being procured were developed at private expense*. For instance, the presence of a copyright has justified a sole source procurement.[61] Proprietary rights in technical data will also justify a sole source procurement. Patented items, however, will not justify a sole source procurement. This is because patent owners

---

(3) procedures established by the Administrator of General Services for the multiple award schedule program, (4) procurements conducted in furtherance of Section 15 of the Small Business Act, and (5) a competitive selection of research proposals resulting from a general solicitation and peer review or scientific review solicited pursuant to Section 9 of the Small Business Act. 10 U.S.C. § 2302(2); 41 U.S.C. § 259(b).

[57] 10 U.S.C. § 2304(j); 41 U.S.C. § 253(h).

[58] 10 U.S.C. § 2305(b)(4)(B); 41 U.S.C. § 253b(d)(2).

[59] 41 U.S.C. § 253(c)(1); 10 U.S.C. § 2304(c)(1).

[60] *Daniel H. Wagner Assocs.*, 65 Comp. Gen. 305 (B-220633), 86-1 CPD ¶ 166.

[61] *ALK Assocs.*, Comp. Gen. Dec. B-237019, 90-1 CPD ¶ 113.

are entitled to reasonable compensation if an invention is used "by or for the United States without a license."[62]

- An *unsolicited proposal* may also provide the basis for a determination that the property or services are available from only one source. In order for this exception to apply, the unsolicited research proposal must demonstrate "a unique and innovative concept the substance of which is not otherwise available to the United States and does not resemble the substance of a pending competitive procurement."[63]

- Sole source contracting is also permitted for *follow-on contracts,* such as those for follow-on buys of major weapon systems.[64]

2. **Unusual and compelling urgency**[65] —This exception to the requirement for full and open competition is based on unusual and compelling urgency. This exception is construed narrowly. It has been applied where the agency made reasonable efforts to obtain competition but was unable to because of insufficient time to fulfill critical agency requirements. For example, the Comptroller General upheld an agency's determination of unusual and compelling urgency in a case where the Marine Corps had determined that only one company was capable of immediately supplying chemical protective suits for use in Operation Desert Storm, the military operation to retake Kuwait.[66]

3. **Industrial mobilization or need to maintain engineering, developmental, or research capability**[67] —This exception permits other than full and open competition to be obtained in order to achieve industrial mobilization or to establish or maintain an essen-

---

[62] 28 U.S.C. § 1498(a).

[63] 41 U.S.C. § 253(d)(1)(A); 10 U.S.C. § 2304(d)(1)(A).

[64] 41 U.S.C. § 253(d)(1)(B); 10 U.S.C. § 2304(d)(1)(B).

[65] 41 U.S.C. § 253(c)(2); 10 U.S.C. § 2304(c)(2).

[66] *Greenbrier Indus., Inc.*, Comp. Gen. Dec. B-241304, 91-1 CPD ¶ 92.

[67] 41 U.S.C. § 253(c)(3); 10 U.S.C. § 2304(c)(3).

tial engineering, research, or development capability to be provided by an educational or other nonprofit institution or a federally funded research and development center. Generally an agency's use of this exception will not be questioned.[68]

4. **International agreement or treaty**[69] —This exception is used when the terms of an international agreement or treaty have the effect of requiring the use of procedures other than competitive procedures.[70]

5. **Statutory authorization or requirement**[71] —Under this exception, the use of other than competitive procedures is permitted when a statute expressly authorizes or requires that a procurement be made through another agency or from a specified source. Usually, sole source awards under the 8(a) set-aside program are justified under this exception.[72]

6. **Risk of compromising the national security**[73] —An agency may use other than competitive procedures if it is determined that the disclosure of the agency's needs would compromise the national security. For example, this exception was appropriately used in the development of "stealth" (i.e., low radar signature) aircraft, where merely disclosing the fact that the military wanted to develop such a technology would have compromised national security and permitted adversaries to begin work on countermeasures immediately.

7. **Protecting the public interest**[74] —This last exception permits the head of an agency to make a determination that it is necessary in

---

[68] *Right Away Foods/Shelf Stable Foods*, Comp. Gen. Dec. B-259859.3, 95-2 CPD ¶ 34.

[69] 41 U.S.C. § 253(c)(4); 10 U.S.C. § 2304(c)(4).

[70] *See Kahn Indus., Inc.*, Comp. Gen. Dec. B-225491, 87-1 CPD ¶ 343.

[71] 41 U.S.C. § 253(c)(5); 10 U.S.C. § 2304(c)(5).

[72] *Bosco Contracting Inc.*, Comp. Gen. Dec. B-236989, 89-2 CPD ¶ 346.

[73] 41 U.S.C. § 253(c)(6); 10 U.S.C. § 2304(c)(6).

[74] 41 U.S.C. § 253(c)(7); 10 U.S.C. § 2304(c)(7).

the public interest to use other than competitive procedures. Congressional notification is required for use of this exception.

It is important to note that, other than the sole source exception, some degree of competition should be obtained whenever circumstances permit.[75] In other words, contracting officers must solicit offers from as many potential sources as is practicable under the circumstances.[76] An agency violation of this provision may occur where it awards a sole source contract under an urgent situation. The urgency may justify the use of other than competitive procedures but a protest may be upheld on the basis that the agency could have obtained *at least some competition*. For example, if special medical test kits are needed immediately for the development of an Army medical unit, the Army would be justified in limiting competition to the two medical suppliers with known stocks of kits on hand, rather than all 10 responsible sources. However, the Army would not be justified in making a sole source award knowing that there were two medical suppliers with known stocks of kits on hand.

B. Methods of Contracting

There are two primary methods of contracting: (1) sealed bidding and (2) competitive negotiation. Because award is based solely on low price and price-related factors, sealed bidding may be used only with a fixed-price-type contract. Negotiated procurement, on the other hand, may be used with any type of contract. There are different sets of rules for the two methods. It is important to understand the differences between these two methods when responding to either a Government solicitation or invitation. In addition to these two primary methods, there are several other methods of contracting, such as micro-purchases, simplified acquisition, and commercial item procurement. There are also five alternative procurement procedures set forth in the statute.[77] In addition to these procedures, some agencies are authorized to use special procurement procedures, and these will be set forth in any agency-specific regulation. The following describes the various methods of contracting. See **Figure 2-1** below for a summary comparison between sealed bid and competitive negotiation.

---

[75] FAR 6.301(d).

[76] *Id.*

[77] 10 U.S.C. § 2302(2); 41 U.S.C. § 259(b).

Figure 2-1 Sealed Bidding vs. Negotiated Procurement--Summary

Characteristics	Sealed Bidding	Negotiated Procurement
Initiating document	Invitation for Bids ("IFB")	Request for Proposals ("RFP") or Request for Quotations ("RFQ")
Response (Offer)	Bid	Proposal
Specifications	Must be precise	Need not be definite
Minimum prospective offers	Two	May be sole source
Late bids or modifications	Considered only if delayed in mail or late primarily because mishandled by Government	Essentially the same
Amendment of solicitation (including specifications) after closing	Not allowed	Allowed
Withdrawal or modifications of offer after closing and before award	Not allowed	Offer may be withdrawn at any time before acceptance and may be modified as permitted
Selection criteria	Award only to low, responsive, and responsible bidder	Award in accordance with stated evaluation criteria (not necessarily low price)
Types of contracts awarded	Only fixed-price	May be fixed-price or cost-reimbursement type

1. Micro-Purchases

Micro-purchases are used for the acquisition of supplies or services (except construction), the aggregate amount of which does not exceed $2,500. Micro-purchases are limited to $2,000 for construction contracts.[78] In making micro-purchases, the Government generally buys commercial items and competitive quotations need not be solicited if the buyer considers the price to be reasonable.[79] Where there is reason to believe the price may be unreasonable, it is resolved by making price comparisons. Generally the Government makes micro-purchases by using a Government-wide commercial credit card,[80] which is a commercial type credit card such as those issued by Visa, American Express or Mastercard.

2. Simplified Acquisition Procedures

The simplified acquisition procedures method is used for making purchases of supplies above $2,500 but not exceeding the simplified acquisition threshold ($100,000). Simplified purchases may be made using imprest funds, purchase orders, blanket purchase agreements, Government-wide commercial purchase cards, or any other authorized method.[81] Unless the products of a small business is not available, all simplified acquisitions are set-aside for small business.[82] In addition, the Government is only required to achieve "maximum practicable competition," not "full and open competition" which means that only a "reasonable number of sources" need be solicited.[83] The FAR states that agencies should consider soliciting at least three sources,[84] and that is generally what agencies solicit in simplified

---

[78] FAR 2.101.

[79] FAR 13.202(a)(2).

[80] FAR 13.201(b); FAR 13.202(a)(2).

[81] FAR 13.301.

[82] FAR 13.003(b)(1).

[83] 41 U.S.C. § 427(c); FAR 13.104.

[84] FAR 13.104(b).

acquisitions. Finally, oral solicitations are encouraged for simplified acquisitions.[85]

3. *Commercial Item Procurements*

FAR 2.101 defines "commercial items" very liberally, to include:

(1) Any item, other than real property, that is of a type customarily used by the general public or by non-governmental entities for purposes other than governmental purposes, and—

    (i) Has been sold, leased, or licensed to the general public; or

    (ii) Has been offered for sale, lease, or license to the general public;

(2) Any item that evolved from an item described in paragraph (1) of this definition through advances in technology or performance and that is not yet available in the commercial marketplace, but will be available in the commercial marketplace in time to satisfy the delivery requirements under a Government solicitation;

(3) Any item that would satisfy a criterion expressed in paragraphs (1) or (2) of this definition, but for—

    (i) Modifications of a type customarily available in the commercial marketplace; or

    (ii) Minor modifications of a type not customarily available in the commercial marketplace made to meet Federal Government requirements. Minor modifications means modifications that do not significantly alter the nongovernmental function or essential physical characteristics of an item or component, or change the purpose of a process. Factors to be considered in determining whether a modification is minor include the value and size of the modification and the comparative value and size of the final product. Dollar values and percentages may be used as guideposts, but are not conclusive evidence that a modification is minor;

(4) Any combination of items meeting the requirements of paragraphs (1), (2), (3), or (5) of this definition that are of a type customarily combined and sold in combination to the general public;

---

[85] FAR 15.203(f).

(5) Installation services, maintenance services, repair services, training services, and other services if—

(i) Such services are procured for support of an item referred to in paragraph (1), (2), (3), or (4) of this definition, regardless of whether such services are provided by the same source or at the same time as the item; and

(ii) The source of such services provides similar services contemporaneously to the general public under terms and conditions similar to those offered to the Federal Government;

(6) Services of a type offered and sold competitively in substantial quantities in the commercial marketplace based on established catalog or market prices for specific tasks performed under standard commercial terms and conditions. This does not include services that are sold based on hourly rates without an established catalog or market price for a specific service performed. For purposes of these services—

(i) Catalog price means a price included in a catalog, price list, schedule, or other form that is regularly maintained by the manufacturer or vendor, is either published or otherwise available for inspection by customers, and states prices at which sales are currently, or were last, made to a significant number of buyers constituting the general public; and

(ii) Market prices means current prices that are established in the course of ordinary trade between buyers and sellers free to bargain and that can be substantiated through competition or from sources independent of the offerors.

(7) Any item, combination of items, or service referred to in paragraphs (1) through (6) of this definition, notwithstanding the fact that the item, combination of items, or service is transferred between or among separate divisions, subsidiaries, or affiliates of a contractor; or

(8) A nondevelopmental item, if the procuring agency determines the item was developed exclusively at private expense and sold in substantial quantities, on a competitive basis, to multiple State and local governments.

The FASA changed the procurement laws and regulations so there is now a preference for commercial items over noncommercial items. The FAR essentially states that agencies shall conduct market research to determine if their needs can be met with commercial items, and if so, the agency must buy commercial items.[86] Agencies are permitted to use sealed bidding or negotiated procurement, and are encouraged to use simplified methods. Contracts for commercial items use a special form (Standard Form ("SF") 1449), and are required to use standard terms and conditions.[87] In addition, there are numerous procurement laws which, by law, are *inapplicable* to commercial item contracts.[88]

Commercial item procurements are not limited to the simplified acquisition threshold of $100,000. A special test program for obtaining commercial items permits an agency to use the commercial item methodology for contracts up to $5 million.[89]

4. *Sealed Bidding*

This method of contracting solicits the submission of competitive bids, through an Invitation for Bids ("IFB"), followed by a public opening of the bids. Award is made to the responsive, responsible bidder whose bid is most advantageous to the Government, considering price and price-related factors. See Section IV below for a detailed discussion.

5. *Competitive Negotiation*

This procedure uses a Request for Proposals ("RFP") or a Request for Quotations ("RFQ") setting out the Government's requirements and the criteria for evaluation of offers. Although the Government may award without conducting any negotiations, this procedure usually provides for discussion or negotiation with those offerors found to be within the competitive range. Award is made to the offeror whose offer is most advantageous

---

[86] FAR 12.101(a); FAR 12.101(b).

[87] FAR 52.212-4, Contract Terms and Conditions—Commercial Items. This clause contains 19 specific provisions that must be used when procuring commercial items.

[88] *See* FAR 12.504.

[89] See FAR 13.500. The authority to issue solicitations under this subpart expires on January 1, 2006. Defense Authorization Act, 2004, Pub. L. No. 108-136, § 1443(b) (Nov. 24, 2003).

to the Government, considering price and the other factors included in the solicitation. See Section V below for a detailed discussion.

6. Architectural and Engineering ("A-E") Services

This special procedure is conducted in two phases. In the first phase, the agency prepares a final selection list of potential contractors, in order of preference, that are considered the most qualified to perform the services based on all relevant criteria except the fee to be paid for the service. In the second phase, the contracting officer negotiates the contract with the most preferred firm on the selection list. If a satisfactory contract cannot be negotiated with this firm, the contracting officer is then permitted to negotiate with the next in the rankings.

7. Competitive Selection of Basic Research Proposals

Under this procedure, research organizations propose to undertake different research tasks in response to periodic announcements (called "broad agency announcements" ("BAAs")) of broad areas of research interest. Agencies review these proposals through a peer or scientific review process and award contracts. The contract runs until funds are exhausted in a particular area. This procedure differs significantly from sealed bidding and competitive negotiation procedures.

8. Multiple Award Schedule Contracts

Multiple award schedule ("MAS") contracts contain standard commercial products and services awarded by the Federal Supply Service of the General Services Administration. These award schedules contain the discounted commercial prices that the listed offerors will charge Government agencies placing orders under them.[90] Buying activities may order directly off the schedules; no competition is required. The Government normally includes a clause requiring that it receive the lowest possible price (i.e., the price sold to the "most favored customer"). In Fiscal Year 2003, agencies purchased goods and services valued at $27.5 billion under MAS contracts. Because of the volume of MAS contracts, a detailed discussion of MAS procedures is in Appendix A of this book.

---

[90] GSAR 538.271(a).

9. Small Business Innovative Research Program

This procedure is the competitive selection of research proposals resulting from a general solicitation and peer or scientific review solicited pursuant to Section 9 of the Small Business Act.[91] Firms with 500 or fewer employees are eligible for participation in the program (nonprofit organizations are excluded).[92]

10. Two-Phase Design-Build Selection Procedures

This is a relatively new procedure enacted by the Clinger-Cohen Act of 1996.[93] Basically under this procedure a contractor is responsible for both the design and the construction of the project. The procedure is known as a two-phase selection procedure. The agency develops a scope of work statement that defines the project and provides prospective contractors with sufficient information regarding the Government's requirements. If the agency contracts for development of the scope of the work statement, then it must contract for A-E services in accordance with the Brooks Architect-Engineers Act.[94]

11. Information Technology

This procedure was established by the Clinger-Cohen Act of 1996.[95] The Act repealed the Brooks Act,[96] which gave the General Services Administration authority over the purchase of information technology ("IT") for the Federal Government. Individual agencies are now authorized to contract directly for IT goods and services.

---

[91] 15 U.S.C. § 638.

[92] 121 C.F.R. § 121.702.

[93] Pub. L. No. 104-106, § 4105, codified at 10 U.S.C. § 2305a and 41 U.S.C. § 253m.

[94] 40 U.S.C. § 541 *et seq.*

[95] Pub. L. No. 104-106, § 5112.

[96] 40 U.S.C. § 759.

12. Other Agency Procedures

In addition to the above-mentioned procedures, some agencies have statutory authority to use special procurement procedures. For instance, NASA uses a MidRange procurement program. This method is considered to be full and open competition[97] and is intended to streamline and expedite the acquisition process. It applies to all acquisitions at NASA the aggregate amount of which is not more than $10 million including options, and for commercial items not more than $25 million including options.[98] It may be used for commercial item contracts above $25 million at the installation's discretion.[99] The Federal Aviation Administration uses two competitive methods. The first method is described under "Complex and Noncommercial Source Selection."[100] This method is used for complex, large-dollar, developmental, and noncommercial items and services. The second method is "Commercial and Simplified Purchase Method" and is used for commercial items that are less complex, small in dollar value and shorter term.[101]

C. Summary: Rules for Competition Requirements and Methods of Contracting

1.   For sealed bidding and competitive negotiation procurements, be aware that offers are solicited on the basis of full and open competition and prepare offers accordingly.

2.   Ensure that a proposal submitted in response to an RFP is competitive and meets the solicitation requirements because the contracting officer can limit the number of proposals in the competitive range to the greatest number that will permit an efficient competition.

---

[97] NFS 1871.104.

[98] NFS 1871.102.

[99] Id.

[100] Federal Aviation Administration Management System 3.2.2.3.

[101] Federal Aviation Administration Management System 3.2.2.5.

3.   Understand that for micro-purchases and simplified acquisitions, only limited competition is required. The standard for simplified acquisition is "maximum practicable competition."

4.   If selling commercial items, obtain a through understanding of the standard contract clause, Contract Terms and Conditions— Commercial Items (FAR 52.212-4), which contains 19 specific provisions to be used in contracts for commercial items.

5.   In any procurement, determine whether there are any unique procurement methods that are specific to the particular agency that is conducting the procurement.

III. TYPES OF CONTRACTS

There are two broad categories of contract types: fixed-price contracts (where the contractor is paid a fixed, known price established when the contract is awarded, including all costs and profit,) and cost-reimbursement contracts (where the contractor is paid for actual costs incurred plus a profit). However, there are a number of variations within each category, and there are some special subsets (indefinite-delivery contracts, time-and-materials contracts, and labor-hour contracts). The amount of payments from the Government could differ significantly depending upon the contract type. It is important that contractors understand the differences in contract types, both when bidding on and when performing Government contracts.

A. Fixed-Price Contracts, Including those with Economic Price Adjustment and those with Incentives

A fixed-price contract calls for one firm price, not subject to any adjustment based on the contractor's cost experience in performance of the contract.[102] A fixed-price contract must be used where a contract results from sealed bidding[103] or where the items being procured are commercial items.[104] Fixed-price contracts are also used where there are definite

---

[102] FAR 16.201.

[103] FAR 16.102.

[104] FAR 12.207.

specifications for the goods or services being acquired and where the contracting officer can establish reasonable and fair prices at the outset of the contract. One variant, the fixed-price contract with economic price adjustment, provides for a firm fixed price that is adjusted upward or downward if certain contingencies occur, e.g., changes in agreed-upon prices of specific items in the contract or changes in the index prices of labor or material. The other variant is the fixed-price-incentive contract, which provides for a firm fixed price but adjusts profit and final contract price by applying a formula based on the relationship of total final cost to total target cost. This type of contract, which is less common, is used where the contract itself can provide an incentive for the contractor to exercise effective cost control.

B. Cost-Reimbursement Contracts, Including those with Fixed Fee, Incentive Fee, and Award Fee

Cost-reimbursement contracts estimate the full cost of the contract ("target cost") for purposes of establishing a ceiling, but provide that the contractor will be paid all allowable costs incurred, to the extent prescribed by the contract and regulations, plus a profit (also known as a "fee").[105] These types of contracts are used only when uncertainties in contract performance do not permit costs to be estimated with sufficient accuracy to use a fixed-price contract (such as the development of high technology weaponry, space launchers, etc.). These contracts generally provide for cost plus fixed fee, with the fee determined when the contract is awarded; a cost plus incentive fee, where a target fee set at award is later adjusted by a formula based on the relationship of total costs to target costs, giving the contractor an incentive to keep costs down; or a cost plus award fee, where the contractor's fee is determined by an award given periodically by a high-ranking official in the procuring agency. A cost-plus-a-percentage-of-cost system of contracting, whereby a contractor is assured of greater profits by incurring higher costs, is prohibited by law.[106]

---

[105] FAR 16.301.

[106] 10 U.S.C. § 2306.

C. Indefinite-Delivery Contracts

Indefinite-delivery contracts are used when the exact times and/or the exact quantities of the deliveries that the Government will require are not known.[107] There are three types of these contracts: (1) definite-quantity contracts, which provide for delivery of a definite quantity during a fixed period, with deliveries to be scheduled upon order from the Government; (2) requirements contracts, which provide that the Government will use the contract to fill *all* of its actual purchase requirements during a specified period, with deliveries to be scheduled by placing orders with a *single* contractor;[108] and (3) indefinite-quantity contracts, which provide for an indefinite quantity, within stated limits, to be furnished during a fixed period with deliveries to be scheduled by placing orders with the contractors. These are known as indefinite-delivery, indefinite-quantity (IDIQ) contracts, which are generally the most common indefinite-delivery contracts. A requirements contract is valid even if the Government places no (zero) orders; an indefinite-quantity contract requires that the Government buy at least the minimum quantity specified in the contract. Furthermore, the minimum quantity in an IDIQ contract must be "more than a nominal quantity, but it should not exceed the amount the Government is fairly certain to order."[109]

Because the quantities that will be purchased by the Government in indefinite-delivery contracts are unknown, the contractor must carefully review all current estimates, attempt to calculate the Government's likely purchase, and develop its offer to minimize risk if the estimated quantities do not materialize.

D. Time-and-Materials and Labor-Hour Contracts

These two types of contracts provide for acquiring supplies or services on the basis of direct labor hours at specified fixed hourly rates (including profit).[110] In a time-and-materials contract, materials (at cost) are also

---

[107] FAR Subpart 16.5.

[108] Compare requirements contracts with commercial requirements contracts as described in Uniform Commercial Code § 2-306.

[109] FAR 16.504(a)(2).

[110] FAR Subpart 16.6.

included in the contract price, whereas in a labor-hour contract, only time (no materials) is included. These types of contracts are used only when it is not possible to estimate accurately the extent or duration of the work or to anticipate costs.

E. Letter Contracts

A letter contract is a written preliminary contract that authorizes the contractor to begin immediately manufacturing supplies or preparing services.[111] It is used when the Government needs to make a binding commitment to the contractor so work can start immediately, but negotiating a complete, full-blown contract is not possible in the time available. The regulations require that the contract be fully definitized within 180 days after the date of the letter contract or before completion of 40 percent of the work to be performed, whichever comes first.[112]

F. Caveats in the Use of Different Types of Contracts and their Formation

Contractors must understand that in general, without a formal contract (including a purchase order, task order or delivery order) signed by a warranted contracting officer, the Government has no obligation to pay for the goods or services.[113] Every contractor should exercise great caution in beginning any work without a formal signed contract. Although oral assurances that are made by a warranted contracting officer who has authority to award a contract *might* be sufficient to bind the Government, assurances from a contracts specialist or any other person who lacks

---

[111] FAR 16.603-1.

[112] FAR 16.603-2(c).

[113] "Contract" means a mutually binding legal relationship obligating the seller to furnish the supplies or services (including construction) and the buyer to pay for them. It includes all types of commitments that obligate the Government to an expenditure of appropriated funds and that, except as otherwise authorized, are in writing. In addition to bilateral instruments, contracts include (but are not limited to) awards and notices of awards; job orders or task letters issued under basic ordering agreements; letter contracts; orders, such as purchase orders, under which the contract becomes effective by written acceptance or performance; and bilateral contract modifications. FAR 2.101.

authority to award a contract *are totally meaningless* and the Government will have no obligation to pay.[114] The best practice is to refrain from beginning any work or incurring any costs until the contractor has a written contract, signed by a contracting officer with proper authority. Contractors should resist all entreaties from any Government official to initiate work prior to obtaining such a written document. Contractors should remind Government officials who cite "urgency" or state that "the contract will be signed in two days" that the Government may use a letter contract to authorize immediate work, bind the Government, and thereby protect the contractor. Even a facsimile copy of a signed contract or a letter contract is likely to be sufficient; the original is not required to begin work.[115]

In addition, before beginning any work on a contract, ensure that funds are available. The contract may state that "no funds are presently available" or it may include FAR 52.232-18, which makes a similar statement. Contractors should not begin work until receiving written assurance by the contracting officer that funds are presently available.

---

[114] The federal circuit recently addressed the issues of oral contracts, holding that if the Government official lacks authority to bind the Government, no contract exists. The court stated:

It is well established that the government is not bound by the acts of its agents beyond the scope of their actual authority. Contractors dealing with the United States must inform themselves of a representative's authority and the limits of that authority. Moreover, "anyone entering into an agreement with the Government takes the risk of accurately ascertaining the authority of the agents who purport to act for the Government, and this risk remains with the contractor even when the Government agents themselves may have been unaware of the limitations on their authority." The burden was on [the contractor] to prove that the [Government official] had the authority to enter into the oral, unilateral contract. The fact that [the contractor] may have believed that the CO had authority is irrelevant; [the contractor] must prove that the [government official] had actual authority.

Harbert/Lummus Agrifuels Projects, et al. v. United States, 142 F.3d 1429, 1432 (Fed.Cir.1998).

[115] Although the Federal Rules of Evidence state a preference for an original document to prove the contents of the contract, Fed. R. Evid. 1002, a duplicate (e.g., a facsimile) is admissible to the same extent unless there is a genuine question about the authenticity of the original or it would be unfair to admit the duplicate in lieu of the original. Fed. R. Evid. 1003.

G. Summary: Rules for Types of Contracts

1.   In preparing bids and proposals in response to Government so-licitations, carefully examine the solicitation to determine the type of contract contemplated, and understand the risks involved in different types of contracts.

2.   When preparing offers on indefinite-quantity contracts, examine current and historical estimates carefully, and remember that significantly greater risk normally requires higher unit prices.

3.   Do not start to perform any contract before receiving a signed copy of the contract award and an indication that funds are presently available for the contract.

4.   If the Government expresses urgency to begin contract performance prior to receiving a signed copy of the contract award, insist that the contracting officer telefax a signed letter contract.

IV. SEALED BIDDING

Sealed bidding is a method of contracting that solicits the submission of competitive bids, followed by a public opening of the bids. Award is made to the responsive and responsible bidder whose bid is most advantageous to the Government, considering price and price-related (e.g., transportation costs) factors.[116]

Sealed bidding *must* be used if all of the following four conditions apply:

- time permits the solicitation, submission, and evaluation of sealed bids;

- the award will be made on the basis of price and other price-related factors (primarily transportation);

- it is not necessary to conduct discussions with the responding sources about their bids; and

---

[116] FAR 14.103-2.

- there is a reasonable expectation of receiving more than one sealed bid.[117]

A. Invitation for Bids

The Government solicits sealed bids through an Invitation for Bids ("IFBs"). An IFB will use the Uniform Contract Format "to the maximum practicable extent."[118] See **Figure 2-2** below. An IFB includes all the terms and conditions of the prospective contract except price. Thus, all bidders will submit bids on the same basis so that award can be made solely on the basis of price and price-related factors. Solicitations are issued on multipurpose standard forms. The contracting officer may use Standard Form ("SF") 33 (Solicitation, Offer and Award), SF 1447 (Solicitation/Contract), SF 1442 (Solicitation, Offer, and Award) for use in construction contracts,[119] SF 1449 (Solicitation/Contract/Order for Commercial Items), or may use a special form.[120] IFBs for contracts over $25,000 must be publicized to prospective bidders. This is done by posting on the Government point of entry ("GPE") on the Internet, at www.fedbizopps.gov.

Where the Government revises its needs or makes an error or includes a defect or ambiguity in the solicitation, the Government must issue SF 30, Amendment of Solicitation/Modification of Contract to amend the solicitation. The amendment must be sent to each concern to whom the IFB has been furnished. However, the bidder bears the risk of not receiving an amendment, unless the failure to receive the amendment is due to a conscious and deliberate effort by the agency to exclude the bidder from the competition.

Virtually every Government contract includes between twenty-five and 100 or more clauses that are "incorporated by reference." When incorporated by reference, clauses have the "same force and effect as if they were given in full text." See FAR 52.252-1. This means that even though the text is not printed in the solicitation (or the resulting contract), both the Government and the contractor are responsible for performing every duty stated in

---

[117] 10 U.S.C. § 2304(a)(2); 41 U.S.C. § 253(a)(2).

[118] FAR 14.201-1(a).

[119] FAR 36.701(b); FAR 53.236-1(e).

[120] FAR 14.201-2(a); FAR 53.214.

Uniform Contract Format	
Part I—The Schedule	
Section	Title
A	Solicitation/contract form
B	Supplies or services and prices/costs
C	Description/specifications/statement of work
D	Packaging and marking
E	Inspection and acceptance
F	Deliveries or performance
G	Contract administration data
H	Special contract requirements
Part II—Contract Clauses	
I	Contract clauses
Part III—List of Documents, Exhibits, and Other Attachments	
J	List of attachments
Part IV—Representations and Instructions	
K	Representations, certifications, and other statements of offerors or respondents
L	Instructions, conditions, and notices to offerors or respondents
M	Evaluation factors for award

Figure 2-2

the full text of the clause. The full text may be obtained by going to the internet (www.arnet.gov/far), or by requesting the text from the contracting officer.

B. Flowdown Provisions to Subcontractors

There are more than 1,000 standard clauses for Government contracts that are reproduced in the FAR, and most contracts include at least 65–100 of these clauses. Certain clauses like the audit clause[121] or the Subcontracts (Labor Standards) clause[122] explicitly require the prime contractor to "flowdown" the particular clause to any subcontractors (i.e., include the clause in all subcontracts). Many other clauses should be flowed down, but the Government fails to so advise the contractor. The best example of these are the Changes clause and the Termination for the Convenience of the Government clause, discussed previously in Chapter 1. It is important that every prime contractor analyze all of its contract clauses and flow any necessary clauses down to subcontractors. *When in doubt, flow the clauses down.* Furthermore, contractors should be absolutely certain to flow down the Changes and Termination for the Convenience of the Government clause. Otherwise they will be stuck with and must pay for completely useless supplier/subcontractor deliveries, if the Government changes or terminates for convenience the contract, and their supplier demands compliance with the subcontract (that is, refuses to make the change desired by the Government).

C. Preparation and Submission of Bids

Prospective bidders must be given a reasonable period of time to prepare and submit bids.[123] A bidding time (i.e., the time between issuance of the solicitation and opening of bids) of at least 30 calendar days must be provided when synopsis is required by FAR Subpart 5.2 (for contract actions that exceed $25,000).[124]

---

[121] FAR 52.215-2.

[122] FAR 52.222-11.

[123] FAR 14.202-1.

[124] *Id.*

In preparing a bid, the bidder should carefully review IFB Section L, Instructions to Offerors, and ensure full compliance with everything mentioned therein. A bidder should prepare a detailed checklist when first reading the IFB. Then, before submitting its bid, the bidder should check its bid against the checklist. The bidder should submit only what is required to the Government, but should be sure to provide everything that was requested. In particular, the bidder should prepare and submit prices on the Government's bid schedule—the bidder should not create or recreate its own schedule through electronic scanning. This may introduce error that may not be correctable. Furthermore, after completion of any bid, it should be carefully checked for all unit prices and mathematical calculations. This should be done by the individual who prepared the bid, as well as by a person who did not prepare the bid.

The contracting officer may extend the bidding time in order to increase competition.[125] Remember though, if the bidding time has not been extended, then the bidder must submit its bid on time.

In preparing bids, the bidder must pay particular attention to the section on representations and certifications. The Government uses representations and certifications for two main purposes: to determine the status of the bidder and to ensure that the bidder will be in compliance with the socioeconomic requirements of the procurement.

Bids must be submitted in accordance with the IFB. For instance, if a bidder transmits its bid by facsimile, and such method is not allowed by the IFB, then the bid will probably not be considered. It does not matter if the bid was received prior to bid opening or even if it was the low bid. Failure to comply with the IFB is usually fatal.

The most common and traditional method of submitting bids is to submit them in a sealed envelope or package addressed to the office specified in the solicitation and showing the time and date specified for receipt, the solicitation number, and the name and address of the bidder.[126] Bids may be transmitted by facsimile *only* if authorized by the solicitation.[127] If facsimile bids are permitted, such bids must be received in the office designated for

---

[125] *Ling Dynamic Sys., Inc.*, Comp. Gen. Dec. B-252091, 93-1 CPD ¶ 407.

[126] FAR 52.214-5(a).

[127] FAR 52.214-5(d).

the receipt of bids before the time set for bid opening. When sending a bid by facsimile, the controlling time for determining when a bid is received by an agency is when the *last* page of the bid is received—not when the transmission begins. Thus, if the last page of the bid is transmitted after the time set for bid opening, the bid will be deemed late and will not be considered.

Bids submitted by electronic commerce will be considered only if the electronic commerce method was specifically stipulated or permitted by the solicitation.[128]

D. Duty of Bidder to Seek Clarification

An ambiguity exists when there are two reasonable interpretations to a solicitation.[129] An ambiguity is either latent (not obvious on the face of the solicitation) or patent (obvious on the face of the solicitation).[130] A patent or glaring ambiguity imposes an affirmative duty on the bidder to seek clarification from the contracting officer prior to submitting its bid.[131] If a bidder fails to seek such clarification, it forfeits the opportunity to rely upon its own unilateral interpretation of the contract.[132] The proper method for obtaining clarification is to a send letter to the contracting officer. See **Figure 2-3**.

If an ambiguity is latent (i.e., not obvious), then future disagreements about its meaning will normally be resolved against the party who drafted the contract.[133] (Virtually all Government contracts are drafted by the

---

[128] FAR 52.214-5(e).

[129] *Aeropace Design & Fabrication, Inc.*, Comp. Gen. Dec. B-278896, 98-1 CPD ¶ 139; *Edward R. Marden Corp. v. United States*, 803 F.2d 701, 705 (Fed. Cir. 1986).

[130] *Malkin Elecs. Int'l, Ltd*, Comp. Gen. Dec. B-228886, 87-2 CPD ¶ 586.

[131] *Enrico Roman, Inc. v. United States*, 2 Cl. Ct. 104 (1983).

[132] *Cherry Hill Sand & Gravel Co. v. United States*, 8 Cl. Ct. 757 (1985); *MWK Int'l, Ltd., Inc. v. United States*, 2 Cl. Ct. 206 (1983).

[133] *Chris Berg, Inc. v. United States*, 455 F.2d 1037 (Ct. Cl. 1972); *Big Chief Drilling Co. v. United States*, 15 Cl. Ct. 295 (1988).

Government.) The one condition here is that the alternative interpretation being raised by the non-drafting party must be reasonable.[134]

It is important to scrutinize every solicitation, and raise, in writing, any provisions that are ambiguous. The Government will respond with a written amendment or other written clarification, if it believes that the issue raised is a real ambiguity in the contract. The failure to raise an ambiguity prior to bidding may significantly damage a contractor in the long run, if it is awarded a contract and the Government disagrees with the contractor concerning a provision that was patently ambiguous.

LETTER TO CONTRACTING OFFICER ASKING FOR CLARIFICATION OF SOLICITATION

ABC Company
Address

Date

Ms. Jane Doe
Contracting Officer
Address

RE: Solicitation No. XYZ-123

Dear Ms. Doe:

Specification AS-3345, which is a part of Solicitation No. XYZ-123, appears to contain an error. Ms. Karen Smith, your Contracting Specialist has advised me by telephone that this specification should read "AS-3347." Would you please confirm this change in specification to me in writing. Thank you.

Respectfully submitted,

Andy Jones, President of ABC, Co.

Cc: Karen Smith, Contracting Specialist

Figure 2-3

---

[134] *William F. Klingensmith, Inc. v. United States*, 205 Ct. Cl. 651, 505 F.2d 1257 (1974) (per curiam).

E. Firm Bid Rule and Modification or Withdrawal of Bid Before Opening

Sealed bids are subject to the firm bid rule. This rule prohibits modification or withdrawal of bids after bid opening. The firm bid rule is incorporated in both Standard Form 33 and Standard Form 1447. These forms provide that if the offer is accepted within 60 days (unless the offeror inserts a different period of time in its bid), then the bidder agrees to hold its offered prices firm and agrees to accept any resulting contract subject to the terms and conditions set forth in the invitation.

Bids may be modified or withdrawn, by any method, anytime prior to "the exact time set for opening of bids."[135] Generally bids are modified or withdrawn by written notice to the office designated in the solicitation. A telegraphic modification or withdrawal is acceptable. If the solicitation authorizes facsimile bids, bids may be modified or withdrawn via facsimile.

F. Bid Opening

All bids are publicly opened at the time and place stated in the IFB. The bid opening officer informs those present that the time for bid opening has arrived and then personally and publicly opens all bids. If practical, the bid opening officer will read the bids aloud to the persons present and then will record the bids on Standard Form 1409,[136] Abstract of Offers. This procedure is known as "bid abstracting," and anyone may obtain a copy of the bid abstract. Because abstracts are available to the public, they will not contain information such as the failure to meet minimum standards of responsibility or any other matter properly exempt from public disclosure. The bid abstract permits a competing contractor to know who is the *apparent* low bidder, and which offeror is most likely to receive award if the abstract is accurate and the low bidder is responsible. Every bidder should request and obtain a bid abstract on every procurement on which it competes. Usually abstracts can be obtained at bid opening. In some cases, the abstract will not be available at bid opening and then the bidder will have to write a letter to the contracting officer requesting the abstract.

---

[135] FAR 14.303(a).

[136] FAR 53.301-1409.

G. Late Bids

Bidders are responsible for submitting bids, and any modifications or withdrawals, "so as to reach the Government office designated in the invitation for bid ("IFB") by the time specified in the IFB."[137]

The late-bid rule provides as follows:

(b)(1) Any bid, modification, or withdrawal of a bid received at the Government office designated in the IFB after the exact time specified for receipt of bids is "late" and will not be considered unless it is received before award is made, the contracting officer determines that accepting the late bid would not unduly delay the acquisition; and—

(i) If it was transmitted through an electronic commerce method authorized by the IFB, it was received at the initial point of entry to the Government infrastructure not later than 5:00 p.m. one working day prior to the date specified for receipt of bids; or

(ii) There is acceptable evidence to establish that it was received at the Government installation designated for receipt of bids and was under the Government's control prior to the time set for receipt of bids.

(2) However, a late modification of an otherwise successful bid, that makes its terms more favorable to the Government, will be considered at any time it is received and may be accepted.[138]

Thus, although there appears to have been some relaxation to the harsh late-bid rule, a bidder should make every effort to ensure that its bid arrives at the bid opening on time. The rule is applied strictly, and a late bid will normally *not* be considered.

Bidders should ensure that bids are treated in a manner consistent with their value. If the potential contract value is $1 million, it makes more sense to send the company's contracts manager to a local (or a distant) city where he or she can hand carry the bid and obtain a timely written receipt, than to trust the mail or a private delivery service.[139] No matter how carefully a bid

---

[137] FAR 14.304(a).

[138] FAR 14.304(b)(2).

[139] The terms and conditions for one overnight carrier contain the following guarantee: "In the event of untimely delivery, [the carrier] will … refund or

is prepared, or how competitive it is, it must arrive on time or it will not be considered unless one of the exceptions applies.

H. Nonconformity and Responsiveness

A bid must comply in all material respects with the IFB.[140] Any bid "that fails to conform to the essential requirements of the solicitation must be rejected."[141] It does not matter whether the material nonconformity is deliberate, or occurs by mistake, or whether the bidder is willing to correct or modify the bid to conform to the IFB. The bid must be rejected. If a contracting officer makes award to a bidder whose bid contains a material nonconformity, the award will be held to be *void ab initio*.[142] Examples of material nonconformities include offering materially different products or services from those solicited in the specifications, failing to agree to the IFB's delivery schedule, limiting the rights of the Government or limiting the bidder's liability to the Government.

Responsiveness is a term of art in sealed bidding that means that the bid conforms to the solicitation. In other words, all bidders must bid on exactly the same work and the same terms and conditions—permitting the selection of the winning bidder solely on the basis of price. A bid that is nonresponsive may not be considered for award by contracting officers and must be rejected. The purpose of this requirement is to enable "bidders to stand on an equal footing and maintain the integrity of the sealed bidding system."[143]

A bid that contains a minor informality or irregularity may still be considered responsive. Examples of minor informalities or irregularities include failure of the bidder to return the number of copies of signed bids required by the IFB, furnish information required on the number of its employees or

---

credit all transportation charges." This means that if the delivery is late, the potential value of the contract will be lost, but the sender will receive the cost of transporting the bid, i.e., the fee for the delivery service, which is typically less than $50. This will be a disappointing consolation prize.

[140] FAR 14.301(a).

[141] FAR 14.404-2(a).

[142] void from the outset.

[143] FAR 14.301(a).

sign its bid but only if the unsigned bid is accompanied by other material indicating the bidder's intention to be bound. In addition, a bidder's failure to acknowledge receipt of an amendment to an IFB is a minor informality, but only if (1) the bid received clearly indicates that the bidder received the amendment or (2) the amendment involves only a matter of form or has either no effect or merely a negligible effect on price, quantity, quality (specifications), or delivery schedule of the item bid upon.[144]

If a bid is found to contain a minor informality or irregularity, and the bid is low, then the contracting officer must make award to that low bidder—regardless of the minor informality or irregularity. The contracting officer may give the bidder an opportunity to cure the deficiency or waive it, whichever is in the best interest of the Government.[145]

I. Responsibility

To be awarded a contract, a bidder must be responsible. Responsibility relates to the status of a prospective contractor—whether it has the capability, tenacity, and perseverance to perform a contract. Contracting officers must make an affirmative determination of responsibility before making an award.[146] In other words, the responsibility of a prospective contractor is judged *as of the time of award and not as of the time of submission of the bid.*

To be responsible, a prospective contractor may not be suspended or debarred for Government contracting, and must meet the following standards—

- Have or be able to obtain adequate financial resources to perform the contract.

---

[144] These are considered to be the four material aspects of a bid. Although there may be many terms in a bid, the price, quantity, quality (specifications), and delivery schedule are most important.

[145] FAR 14.405.

[146] FAR 9.103(b).

- Be able to comply with the required or proposed delivery or performance schedule, taking into consideration all existing commercial and Government business commitments.

- Have a satisfactory performance record.

- Have a satisfactory record of integrity and business ethics.

- Have or be able to obtain the necessary organization, experience, accounting and operational controls, and technical skills.

- Have or be able to obtain the necessary production, construction, and technical equipment and facilities.

- Be otherwise qualified and eligible to receive an award under applicable laws and regulations.[147]

The contracting officer may use information available to him or her, or may request a preaward survey, which addresses all of these factors.[148] In a preaward survey, one or more Government officials with expertise in finance, production, construction, etc. will usually visit the contractor, examine its facilities and records, and make a recommendation to the contracting officer.

J. Difference Between Responsiveness of Bid and Responsibility of Bidder

It is important to understand the difference between responsiveness and responsibility. Responsiveness deals with whether the contractor *has promised to do exactly what the Government has requested*. Responsibility, on the other hand, has to do with whether the contractor can or will perform as it has promised. Another way to grasp these concepts is to understand that they come up at different periods of time. The question of responsiveness of a bid is determined on the basis of information submitted with the bid and on the facts available at the time of bid opening. Responsibility determinations

---

[147] FAR 9.104-1(g).

[148] FAR 9.106.

of bidders are made on the basis of all information that may be submitted or available about that bidder up to the time of award.

K. Evaluation and Award

In sealed bidding, award must be made to the bidder that submitted a responsive bid, is responsible, and offers the *lowest price*.

The evaluation process in sealed bidding is much more straightforward than in negotiated procurement. Meet the above criteria and you win. Tradeoffs are not permitted. Thus, the Government cannot decide that it is willing to pay more in order to get something more than it had originally asked for in the IFB. Also, discussions between the Government and the bidder are not allowed. The award must be made to a responsible bidder on the basis of the IFB. The contracting officer cannot change the terms in the IFB for the low bidder.

A contracting officer can only make an award if he or she determines that the price of the contract as awarded is reasonable.[149] If all bids are at unreasonable prices, the contracting officer must cancel the solicitation. This is one of the compelling reasons set forth in the FAR for canceling an invitation.[150] In determining whether an offered price is reasonable the contracting officer will conduct a price analysis and look at such things as Government estimates, past procurement history, and current market conditions.[151]

L. Cancellation of IFBs After Bid Opening

A procurement may be canceled after bid opening only if there is a compelling reason to reject all bids and cancel the invitation.[152] Whether a

---

[149] All contracts awarded by sealed bidding must be fixed price (this includes fixed price with economic price adjustment). Sealed bidding may not result in a cost-reimbursement contract.

[150] FAR 14.404-1(c)(6).

[151] *Bay Cities Refuse Serv., Inc.*, Comp. Gen. Dec. B-250807, 93-1 CPD ¶ 151.

[152] FAR 14.404-1(a)(1).

compelling reason exists for bid cancellation is "primarily within the discretion of the administrative agency and will not be disturbed absent proof that the decision was clearly arbitrary, capricious, or not supported by substantial evidence."[153] The regulations require cancellation when the agency finds that it has not properly disclosed the identity or availability of the necessary specifications.[154] Other examples include:

- All bids are at unreasonable prices;

- Inadequate or ambiguous specifications in the invitation;

- Specifications have been revised;

- The supplies or services being contracted for are no longer required;

- The invitation did not provide for consideration of all factors of cost to the Government, such as cost of transporting Government-furnished property to bidders' plants; or

- For other reasons, cancellation is clearly in the public's interest.[155]

M. Mistakes

Bidders are often frenzied and in a rush to submit their bids on time and, as a result, frequently make mistakes. What happens when a mistake is discovered—should a bidder be allowed to correct its mistake? The answer depends on the nature of the mistake.

The first thing to understand is the type of mistakes that are covered by the rules and for which relief is permitted. There is a difference between clerical and arithmetical mistakes and mistakes in judgment. Clerical or arithmetical errors are the most common types of mistakes for which relief is

---

[153] *Ace-Federal Reporters, Inc.*, Comp. Gen. Dec. B-237414, 90-1 CPD ¶ 144.

[154] FAR 14.404-1(b).

[155] FAR 14.404-1(c).

granted. Clerical or arithmetical errors include numbers transposed on a bid document,[156] cost of several items omitted from recap sheets,[157] dividing rather than multiplying in making metric conversion,[158] error in pagination resulting in failure to include estimated costs on one page of estimating sheets,[159] using incorrect number of square feet to calculate the unit price,[160] or omitting a zero when transcribing from worksheet to final bid.[161]

An error in business judgment is not a mistake. When a bidder makes a business judgment, it assumes responsibility for that judgment—even if the bidder's reasoning is flawed.

One category where it is often difficult to discern whether it was a mistake or error in business judgment is the misreading of specifications. Generally it will not be considered to be an error in business judgment when it involves the quantity or nature of work rather than the effort required to perform the work. On the other hand, where a bidder makes a judgment as to the amount of effort or the cost that is required to perform the work, that will be deemed to be an error in business judgment and relief will not be available.

After the opening of bids, contracting officers must examine all bids for mistakes. Once a contracting officer is on notice of a possible mistake, he or she must request verification of the bid and disclose the particular reasons that led to the request.[162] If the contracting officer does not inform the bidder as to why an error might have been made, then the request will be found to be inadequate.[163] For instance, a form letter that did not tell the bidder of the

---

[156] *McCarthy Corp. v. United States*, 204 Ct. Cl. 768, 499 F.2d 633 (1974).

[157] *Allen L. Bender, Inc.*, LBCA 80-BCA-103, 81-2 BCA ¶ 15,435.

[158] *Columbia Pac. Constr., Co.*, Comp. Gen. Dec. B-207313, 82-1 CPD ¶ 436.

[159] *PK Contractors, Inc.*, Comp. Gen. Dec. B-205482, 82-1 CPD ¶ 368.

[160] *Michaels Constr. Co.*, Comp. Gen. Dec. B-257764, 94-2 CPD ¶ 176.

[161] *Pipeline Constr., Inc.*, Comp. Gen. Dec. B-256799, 94-2 CPD ¶ 21.

[162] FAR 14.407-3(g)(1).

[163] *United States v. Hamilton Enters., Inc.*, 711 F.2d 1038 (Fed. Cir. 1983).

gross disparity between its bid and that of the next lowest bidder or the Government funding estimate was found to be inadequate.[164]

In general, both the existence of the mistake and the bid actually intended must be established by clear and convincing evidence in order to correct a bid.[165] However, after bid opening, a bidder may be permitted to withdraw its bid upon the discovery of a mistake as long as the evidence "reasonably supports the existence of a mistake."[166] Remember that a bidder may withdraw its bid at anytime *prior* to bid opening.

N. Summary: Rules for Sealed Bidding

1. Use all available sources for obtaining IFBs, including the Internet (fedbizzopps.gov and agency sites), agency mailing lists, and bulletin boards.

2. Become familiar with the Uniform Contract Format, and understand where to look for various terms and conditions in a contract.

3. When reviewing an IFB, prepare a detailed checklist of all necessary items, paying special attention to Section L, Instructions to Offerors. Prior to submitting the bid, double check that the bid complies fully with the checklist.

4. Check all calculations, unit and extended prices, and all mathematics in the bid.

5. If there are any specifications, terms or portions of the IFB that are ambiguous or unclear, write a letter to the contracting officer requesting clarification.

6. Print all prices in the spaces provided on the IFB pricing schedule—do not create or recreate the IFB's pricing schedule because this might introduce errors.

---

[164] *Chemtronics, Inc.*, ASBCA 30883, 88-2 BCA ¶ 20,534.

[165] FAR 14.407-3(a).

[166] FAR 14.407-3(c)(2).

7. Submit only what is required to the Government in accordance with Section L of the IFB.

8. Read every representation and certification carefully and truthfully execute them.

9. Prior to signing the bid, telephone the contracting officer to confirm that all amendments have been received.

10. Ensure that all amendments to the IFB have been acknowledged.

11. Do not take any exceptions to the terms of the IFB and ensure that the bid is fully responsive to the IFB. Also, ensure that the bid agrees to hold offered prices firm for the period required by the IFB (normally 60 days).

12. Do not enclose any explanatory letters in the bid package.

13. Sign the bid on the cover sheet and sign every required certification.

14. Submit the bid in the manner permitted by the IFB.

15. Submit a bid by facsimile or by electronic means only if it is authorized by the IFB.

16. When submitting a facsimile or electronic bid, ensure that the *last page* is received by the receiving office prior to the opening time stated in the bid. Confirm receipt by telephone.

17. Obtain a signed acknowledgment that the bid was properly received before the bid opening time.

18. Upon discovering a mistake prior to bid opening, send a signed amendment to the bid and make sure it arrives prior to the time specified for bid opening.

19. Attend the bid opening and take extensive notes.

20. Make an immediate request for a copy of the bid abstract. If the abstract is not available at bid opening, request it in writing from the contracting officer immediately thereafter.

21. Retain all bid preparation documentation in case a mistake must be proved after bid opening.

V. NEGOTIATED PROCUREMENT

A. Background

Prior to the enactment of CICA, contracting agencies were required by law[167] to obtain competition through the use of "formal advertising" (now called "sealed bidding") whenever feasible and practicable. Negotiated procurement at that time was considered to be a noncompetitive method that could be used only after the agency had executed a determination and findings concluding that one of 17 statutory exceptions to formal advertising was applicable. The exceptions included such things as a public exigency, an inability to draft adequate specifications, services for which it was impracticable to secure competition or providing for immediate repair to a ship where it was necessary so the ship could comply with its military orders.

With the enactment of CICA, the former statutory preference for sealed bidding was eliminated. Under CICA, with certain limited exceptions, contracting officers are required to promote and provide for full and open competition in soliciting offers and awarding Government contracts.[168] Sealed bidding and competitive proposals (negotiated procurement), as described in FAR Parts 14 and 15 respectively, are both acceptable procedures for achieving full and open competition.[169] However, these are considerably different procurement methods, and yield different results to both the Government and competitors.

In sealed bidding procurements, award must be made to the responsible offeror submitting the lowest offer based on price and price-related factors (such as transportation costs). The system is rigid and the Government has

---

[167] 10 U.S.C. § 2304(a).

[168] FAR 6.101(a).

[169] FAR 6.401.

little flexibility. In negotiated procurement, the Government has much greater flexibility in structuring the procurement, and most importantly, in making the award decision. The Government can consider, in addition to price, other factors such as technical capabilities, past performance of a contractor, or qualifications of key contractor personnel. The Government need not make award to the lowest price offeror, as explained below.

CICA recognized the benefits of negotiated procurements. The National Performance Review conducted by Vice President Gore specifically recommended that agencies use negotiated "best value" procurements.[170] The FAR was revised to state that best value "means the expected outcome of an acquisition that, in the Government's estimation, provides the greatest overall benefit in response to the requirement.[171] The passage of the Clinger-Cohen Act of 1996 and The Federal Acquisition Streamlining Act of 1994 encouraged the use of negotiated best value procurements by mandating the use of past performance and other quality indicators as source selection factors. Subsequently, these requirements were included in the FAR, along with a commitment to purchase through a best value process in negotiated procurement.[172]

Contracting officers have considerable discretion in the type of competitive procedure to be used in any procurement, and are permitted to use negotiated procurements if any of the four requirements for conducting a sealed bid procurement is not present (i.e., there is adequate time, award will be based on price and price related factors only, no discussions with offerors are needed, and more than one offer is expected to be received).

---

[170] National Performance Review, "From Red Tape to Results: Creating a Government That Works Better & Costs Less" Recommendation PROC15 ("Encourage Best Value Procurement") (1993).

[171] FAR 2.101.

[172] *See, e.g.* FAR 15.304(c)(2), which requires that every solicitation for a negotiated procurement include quality of the product or service as an evaluation factor utilizing such subfactors as past performance, technical excellence, management capability, prior experience and compliance with solicitation requirements. *See also* FAR. 15.101, which defines the best value continuum, and FAR 15.302 which states that the "objective of source selection is to select the proposal that represents the best value."

Negotiated procurements have become the preferred method of achieving full and open competition. In Fiscal Year 2002, twelve times as much in contract value was awarded through negotiated competitive procurement as compared with sealed bidding. Using the negotiated best value procurement method instead of sealed bidding permits the Government to award to a higher-priced offeror that offers a commensurately higher-quality product or service, as long as the factors to be used in evaluation of the proposals are clearly stated in the solicitation. This provides the Government with far greater flexibility, and permits higher-priced awards than would be permitted under sealed bidding. However, the benefit of the higher price must be justified by the agency using these techniques, and presumably, results in greater overall value to the Government.

B. Best Value Source Selection Processes and Techniques

Negotiation acquisitions are initiated through the issuance of a solicitation known as a Request for Proposals ("RFP"). The negotiated procurement may be used to contract on a sole source or a competitive basis. Sole source acquisitions are permitted where the supplies or services are available from only one responsible source.[173] Competitive negotiated acquisitions involve a comprehensive evaluation of each offeror's proposal, leading to selection of the one that represents the best value to the Government.

The regulations permit the use of two different types of best value negotiated procurements, or combinations of these methods. The first and most commonly used is a tradeoff process, where it is in the best interest of the Government to consider award to other than the lowest-priced offer, or other than the highest technically rated offeror. In this process, the evaluation factors must be clearly stated in the RFP and the RFP must explain whether the evaluation factors other than cost or price are significantly more important than, approximately equal to, or significantly less important than cost or price. This process permits tradeoffs among cost or price and non-cost factors, and allows the Government to accept other than the lowest-priced proposal, *provided the benefits of the higher-priced proposal merits the additional cost and the rationale for the tradeoff is adequately documented.*[174] The second type of best value procurement is known as the

---

[173] 10 U.S.C. § 2304(c); 41 U.S.C. § 253(c)(1); and FAR 6.302-1(a).

[174] FAR 15.101-1(c).

lowest-priced, technically acceptable ("LPTA") source selection process. This method is used less frequently than the tradeoff process.[175] Here the RFP must state the evaluation factors, and the acceptability standards for each factor. Award is made to the lowest evaluated price proposal that meets or exceeds the standards, and no tradeoffs are allowed. An LPTA process is somewhat similar to sealed bidding in that price becomes the determining factor. However, in LPTA there is an evaluation of the quality of the proposal to ensure that it is technically acceptable and there may be discussions between the Government and the offerors, neither of which is permitted in sealed bidding.

C. The Solicitation—Request for Proposals

RFPs are used in negotiated acquisitions to communicate Government requirements. Before issuing an RFP, agencies are encouraged to exchange information with industry concerning the feasibility of requirements, delivery schedules, performance requirements, statements of work, etc. This process may include issuance of draft RFPs or Requests for Information ("RFI").[176]

With a few minor exceptions, the RFP utilizes the same Uniform Contract Format that is used in sealed bidding.[177] The RFP must include the following:[178]

1.   The Government's requirement;

2.   All anticipated terms and conditions that will apply to the contract. The RFP may authorize offerors to propose alternative terms and conditions, including the Contract Line Item Number ("CLIN") structure;

---

[175] The principal reason for the disparity is because LPTA is an "all or nothing process." An offer that receives an "acceptable" technical score of 60 points, for example, will be compared on equal grounds with an offer with a technical score of 95 points. There can be no distinction between "good" and "outstanding" proposals; both are "technically acceptable."

[176] FAR 15.201(c).

[177] FAR 15.204.

[178] FAR 15.203.

3. All information required to be in the offeror's proposal, which is normally explained in Section L of the RFP, "Instructions, Conditions and Notices to Offerors or Respondents;" and

4. Factors and significant subfactors that will be used to evaluate the proposal, and their relative importance, which are included in Section M of the RFP, "Evaluation Factors For Award." These factors and subfactors must represent key areas of importance in the selection and support meaningful comparison between proposals.[179] Price or cost must be evaluated in *every* source selection,[180] and must be worth at least 10 percent of the evaluation.[181] Furthermore, the quality of the product or service must be evaluated in every source selection through the use of past performance, technical excellence, management capability, personnel qualifications or prior experience. Past performance must be evaluated in all competitive acquisitions over $100,000.[182]

In the same manner as in sealed bidding, the Government is required to issue written amendments to the RFP whenever the Government changes its requirements.

In preparing their proposals, offerors should carefully follow the requirements of Section L, "Instructions to Offerors." Any page limits must be strictly adhered to, since the Government is not required to read beyond any limit.[183] Upon first reading of the RFP, every requirement should be annotated in a checklist, and the final proposal compared with the checklist to ensure that every requirement has been fully and completely addressed.

In developing both a price and technical proposal, the offeror should pay close attention to the evaluation factors in Section M of the RFP, the relative weight that will be given to each factor, and the technical factors in relation

---

[179] FAR 15.304(b).

[180] FAR 15.304(c)(1).

[181] *Boeing Sikorsky Aircraft Support*, Comp. Gen. Dec. B-277263, 97-2 CPD ¶ 91.

[182] FAR 15.304(c)(3)(ii).

[183] *All Star Maintenance, Inc.*, Comp. Gen. Dec. B-244143, 91-2 CPD ¶ 294.

to price. Although the exact percentage weights for each evaluation factor need not be given in the RFP, an offeror can usually determine what the relative percentages are from Section M. In a best value procurement involving a cost/technical tradeoff, if the solicitation fails to explicitly state the relative weight of cost in the evaluation scheme, cost and technical considerations will be accorded equal weight and importance in the evaluation.[184] Some typical evaluation schemes are as follows:

1. Award will be made on a best value, cost/technical tradeoff. All technical factors are of equal weight. All of the technical factors combined are worth more than price.

2. Award will be made on a best value, cost/technical tradeoff. All technical factors are of equal weight. Price is worth more than all of the technical factors combined.

3. Award will be made on a best value, cost/technical tradeoff. All technical factors are of equal weight. Price shall be equal in weight to all of the technical factors combined.

4. Award will be made to the offeror submitting the offer determined to be most advantageous to the Government, and the following are the evaluation factors in descending order of importance: (1) price; (2) technical capability; and (3) past performance. Technical capability and past performance are approximately equal in importance, and technical capability and past performance combined are approximately equal in importance to price.[185]

5. Award will be made using a best value evaluation scheme, considering the following four factors: (1) past and present performance; (2) contractor quality control plan; (3) technical quality (oral presentation); and (4) price/cost. The relative weights of these factors are as follows: Factors 1 and 2 are equal and, individually, are

---

[184] *Meridian Corp.*, Comp. Gen. Dec. B-246330.3, 93-2 CPD ¶ 29.

[185] *Teleport Communications Group*, Comp. Gen. Dec. B-277926, 98-2 CPD ¶ 72. Although the percentages for each factor are not given, it can be inferred that price is worth approximately 50 percent while technical capability and past performance are each worth 25 percent.

less important than factor 3, and factors 1, 2, and 3 are more important than factor 4.[186]

Offerors are required to submit offers so that they reach the Government office designated in the RFP on time. Any proposal that is not received on time is "late" and may be considered only if it is received before the award is made, and it meets essentially the same conditions for lateness as in sealed bidding, i.e., the contracting officer determines that accepting the late offer would not unduly delay the acquisition and (1) if it was transmitted through an electronic commerce method, it was received at the initial point of entry to the Government infrastructure not later than 5:00 p.m. one working day prior to the date specified for receipt of proposals or (2) there is acceptable evidence to establish that it was received at the Government installation designated for receipt of offers and was under the Government's control prior to the time set for receipt of offers.[187] There is one additional exception that is not in sealed bidding. A late offer may also be considered if the contracting officer determines that accepting the late offer would not unduly delay the acquisition and it is the only proposal received.[188]

Unlike sealed bidding procurements, an offeror may withdraw its proposal *any time prior to award*, even after the Government has completed its evaluation.[189]

The RFP is required to include a clause[190] that permits the Government to make award without holding any discussions with offerors. Only if the Government intends to hold discussions may the agency include a clause stating that a competitive range will be established and the contracting officer intends to hold discussions.[191] In addition to these clauses concerning discussions, the agency must include the audit clause[192] except for contracts

---

[186] *Trifax Corp.*, Comp. Gen. Dec. B-279561, 98-2 CPD ¶ 24.

[187] FAR 52.215-1(c)(3)(ii)(A).

[188] FAR 52.215-1(c)(3)(ii)(A)(3).

[189] FAR 15.208(e).

[190] FAR 52.215-1.

[191] FAR 52.215-1 Alt I.

[192] FAR 15.209(b).

not exceeding the simplified acquisition threshold of $100,000, the acquisition of commercial items, and certain other specific exemptions.

Finally, the RFP may provide for the submission of oral proposals, either in addition to, or as a substitute for all or part of the written proposals. These may be used at any time in the acquisition process, and provide the Government with an opportunity to obtain face-to-face clarifications, or to "interview" key personnel on service contracts. Oral presentations provide for a streamlined source selection process.[193] Offerors must exercise great care in preparing for orals, going through "dry-runs" and carefully training the oral presenter. Even where orals are not given a specific evaluation weight, the impressions reached by Government evaluation officials may be heavily influenced by the offeror's performance during orals.

D. Source Selection

Responsibility for making the source selection rests with the agency head, who normally appoints a Source Selection Authority ("SSA") to carry out the source selection. The contracting officer may be designated as the SSA.[194] As noted previously, the objective of source selection is to select the source whose proposal represents the best value to the Government.

1. Award Without Discussions

Once received by the Government, all proposals are evaluated to assess their relative qualities solely on the factors and subfactors specified in the solicitation.[195] Both cost and price as well as technical qualities are evaluated in negotiated procurements. This is normally done by evaluation committees, or by the contracting officer. Evaluations may be conducted using any rating method or combination of methods, including such things as color ratings (blue=outstanding, green=good, yellow=not acceptable but correctable, red=not acceptable and unlikely to be correctable); adjectival ratings (outstanding, excellent, good, acceptable, unacceptable); numerical

---

[193] FAR 15.102.

[194] FAR 15.303.

[195] FAR 15.305.

weights (80 points out of 100 possible; 850 points out of 975 possible); or ordinal rankings (1st, 2d, 3d, etc.).[196]

The Government's evaluation of each proposal includes an assessment of its relative strengths, deficiencies, significant weaknesses and risks, each of which must be documented.[197] The following definitions are important:

- Deficiency is a material failure of a proposal to meet a Government requirement or a combination of significant weaknesses in a proposal that increases the risk of unsuccessful contract performance to an unacceptable level.

- Weakness is a flaw in the proposal that increases the risk of unsuccessful contract performance. A "significant weakness" is a flaw that appreciably increases the risk of unsuccessful contract performance.[198]

Cost or price must be evaluated separately from technical scores. Just as in sealed bidding, a contracting officer may only award a contract if he or she determines that the price is reasonable.[199] Since competition normally establishes price reasonableness, a firm-fixed-price contract (or one with an economic price adjustment) can be compared with other proposed contract prices to perform a price analysis that will confirm reasonableness, and a cost analysis (analysis of the individual cost elements) need not be performed. However, when the contract to be awarded will be a cost-reimbursement contract, where the Government must pay all reasonable, allowable and allocable costs, agencies must performed a cost realism analysis to determine what the Government should realistically expect to pay for the proposed effort, *and only the realistic cost should be used in any cost comparisons or cost/technical tradeoffs.*[200]

During the course of the technical or cost evaluation, the Government may request clarifications from the offerors without holding formal discus-

---

[196] *Id.*

[197] *Id.*

[198] FAR 15.001.

[199] FAR 15.404-1(a).

[200] FAR 15.305(a)(1).

sions. Clarifications are limited exchanges between the Government and offerors whereby the offeror may resolve minor or clerical errors, or discuss the relevance of certain past performance information.[201] However, exchanges for the purposes of clarification may not to be used to cure proposal deficiencies or material omissions, materially alter the technical or cost elements of the proposal, or otherwise revise the proposal.[202] They are strictly for clarification purposes.

After the Government completes its evaluation of both the proposal and the price or cost, the agency may then complete its best value analysis (either LPTA or a cost/technical tradeoff) and make the award without any discussions, if doing so is in the best interest of the Government. Presumably, if the proposals contain deficiencies or weaknesses, it will not be in the best interest of the Government to make award without conducting discussions, and permitting the proposals to be revised to correct such deficiencies or weaknesses. This is a matter that is up to the discretion of the contracting officer, who decides whether to hold discussions.

2.   *Establishing the Competitive Range and Holding Discussions*

If the contracting officer decides that discussions are required in order to achieve best value, the agency must establish a "competitive range," which consists of all of the most highly rated proposals.[203] However, before establishing a competitive range, the agency may conduct limited communications with offerors whose placement in the competitive range is uncertain, or whose past performance information is the determining factor preventing them from being placed in the competitive range.[204] In order to enhance Government understanding and facilitate the evaluation process, the agency may communicate with the offerors, *but may not use these communications* to cure proposal deficiencies or material omissions, materially alter the

---

[201] FAR 15.306(a).

[202] FAR 15.306(b)(2).

[203] FAR 15.306(c)(1).

[204] FAR 15.306(b)(1).

technical or cost elements, or otherwise permit the offeror to revise its proposal.[205]

In establishing the competitive range, the contracting officer must include all of the most highly rated proposals, unless he or she determines that the competitive range must be limited in number for the purposes of efficiency (i.e., there are many proposals in the competitive range, the procurement is complex, it would be more efficient to deal with only the highest three or four offerors).

When the competitive range is established, the contracting officer must notify those offerors that have been excluded, and such offerors may request a debriefing, explaining why they were excluded.[206] If excluded from the competitive range, it is always advisable to request a debriefing in order to assist in future proposal preparation. Requests must be made in writing to the contracting officer within three days after the offeror receives its notice of exclusion from the competitive range. In the debriefing, the agency must tell the offeror: (1) its evaluation of significant elements in the offeror's proposal; (2) the rationale for the offeror's exclusion; and (3) reasonable responses to relevant questions about whether regulations were followed in the exclusion from the competitive range. The agency is prohibited from revealing the number of offerors, the identity of the other offerors, the contents of any other offeror's proposal, the ranking of offerors, or the evaluation of other proposals.[207]

Once the competitive range is established, the contracting officer will conduct exchanges with offerors through written, oral, or a combination of written and oral exchanges. The contracting officer must indicate to, or discuss with each offeror in the competitive range, the significant weaknesses, deficiencies and other aspects of its proposal (such as cost, price, technical approach, past performance, technical approach, and terms and conditions) that could, in the opinion of the contracting officer, be altered or explained to enhance materially the proposal's potential for award.[208] Discussions must be meaningful, equitable and not prejudicially misleading.

---

[205] FAR 15.306(b)(2).

[206] FAR 15.306(c)(3) and (4).

[207] FAR 15.505(f).

[208] FAR 15.306(d)(3).

They must raise issues that concern deficiencies and weaknesses and not conceal deficiencies and weaknesses.[209] The Government may not favor one offeror over another, reveal an offeror's technical solution to another, or reveal an offeror's price without that offeror's permission, or reveal the names of individuals who have provided past performance information.[210] No offeror should permit a contracting officer to reveal its price to another offeror.

During discussions, the contracting officer may request "interim" proposal revision(s) from any offeror at any time in order to reflect understandings reached during negotiations.[211] At the conclusion of discussions, every offeror still in the competitive range[212] must be given an opportunity to revise their offer and submit a single final proposal, making any revision deemed appropriate or necessary by the offeror. The contracting officer must establish a common cut-off date for receipt of the final proposal revisions from all offerors in the competitive range.[213]

Discussions are extremely important as a way to improve a proposal. Every identified deficiency or weakness should be addressed by the offeror in its final proposal revision. During the actual discussions, offerors should make every attempt to determine how best to improve their chances for award. When final proposal revisions are made, offerors should ensure that every required correction or revision has been made, and that their cost proposal has been adjusted. Typically an offeror will submit in its final proposal the lowest cost or price that it can feasibly charge the Government. Frequently, the final proposal is lower in cost or price than the original one. However, offerors may increase their final prices as well, as in the case where certain important items were initially omitted from the proposal, but were added back as a result of discussions. Finally, it is normally inadvisable to make significant technical changes in the proposal that were not identified

---

[209] *Du and Assoc.,* Comp. Gen. Dec. B-280283, 98-2 CPD ¶ 156.

[210] FAR 15.306(e).

[211] FAR 15.307(b).

[212] The Government may drop offerors from the competitive range at any time during discussions if the offeror is no longer considered to be among the most highly rated offerors. FAR 15.306(d)(5).

[213] FAR 15.307(b). Final proposal revisions were previously known as best and final offers (BAFOs).

as deficiencies or weaknesses by the Government. Changes in these areas could create new and unexpected deficiencies or weaknesses, and cause the Government to downgrade a technical proposal.

The Government next re-evaluates the final proposals, based on a comparative assessment of proposals against the source selection criteria in the solicitation, performs a best value analysis (LPTA assessment or cost/technical tradeoff), documents the contract file to explain the rationale for the selection, makes the award decision, and notifies the awardee and the unsuccessful offerors.[214]

E. Award to a Responsible Contractor

Prior to actually awarding the contract, the contracting officer must determine that the intended awardee is responsible, i.e., that it has adequate financial resources to perform the contract, can meet the delivery schedule, has a satisfactory performance and integrity/business ethics records, has the necessary organization, technical skills, production facilities and equipment, and is qualified to obtain the award.[215] The contracting officer must make an affirmative determination of responsibility. In the absence of information clearly indicating that the contractor is responsible, the contracting officer must deem that contractor nonresponsible.[216] The determination of the offeror's responsibility is done in the same manner for a negotiated procurement as it is in sealed bidding (see previous section). The contracting officer may use information available to him or her, or may request a preaward survey, which addresses all of these factors.[217]

---

[214] FAR 15.308.

[215] FAR 9.104-1.

[216] FAR 9.103(b). If the contractor is a small business, determinations of responsibility must be referred to the Small Business Administration ("SBA") for a Certificate of Competency ("COC"). FAR Subpart 19.6. A COC is a complete and independent examination by the SBA of the contractor's responsibility.

[217] FAR 9.106.

The contracting officer's signature on the contract represents his or her affirmative determination of present responsibility of the offeror.[218]

F. Debriefings of Unsuccessful Offerors

As explained previously, any offeror that was not included in the competitive range, or dropped from the competitive range, may request a preaward debriefing.[219] The contents of the preaward debriefing is discussed above.

Far more important to offerors who were included in the competitive range but did not receive the award is the postaward debriefing of offerors. *Every offeror should request a debriefing on any negotiated procurement that was lost in order to assist it in obtaining future awards.* The unsuccessful offeror must make a written request for a debriefing within three days after the date on which it received notice of the contract award, and the Government should give the debriefing, to the maximum extent practicable, within five days after the agency receives the written request.[220] The failure to request a debriefing within three days makes it possible for the agency to deny the unsuccessful offeror a debriefing, should the contracting officer so choose.[221]

Debriefings may be done orally or in writing, by telephone or in person, and the contracting officer normally chairs the debriefing with support from personnel from the evaluation team.[222] The debriefing must include, at a minimum, the following information:

1. The Government's evaluation of the significant weaknesses or deficiencies in the offeror's proposal.

---

[218] FAR 9.105-2(a)(1).

[219] FAR 15.505.

[220] FAR 15.506(a).

[221] FAR 15.506(a)(4)(i).

[222] FAR 15.506(a)(4)(ii)(b) & (c).

2. The overall evaluated cost or price (including unit prices) and technical rating of the successful offeror and the debriefed offeror, and past performance information on the debriefed offeror.

3. The overall ranking of all offerors, when any ranking was developed by the agency (this is frequently *not* developed by agencies).

4. A summary of the rationale for award.

5. For acquisitions of commercial items, the make and model of the item to be delivered by the successful offeror.

6. Reasonable responses to relevant questions about whether source selection procedures and rules were followed.[223]

The debriefing may not include point-by-point comparisons of the debriefed offeror's proposal with those of other offerors, nor may it disclose trade secrets, privileged and confidential commercial or financial information (such as indirect costs or profit) or the names of those who provided past performance information.[224]

G. Contract Pricing and Defective Pricing

Negotiated procurements require that the Government adhere to certain cost and price negotiation policies. Contracting officers must purchase supplies and services at fair and reasonable prices.[225] In order to do so, in a negotiated procurement a contracting officer frequently requires information not normally needed in sealed bidding, where price and price-related factors are the basis of the award and competition generally ensures that prices are reasonable. In a negotiated procurement, the contracting officer needs data underlying the contract price to determine price reasonableness.

---

[223] FAR 15.506(d).

[224] FAR 15.506(e).

[225] FAR 15.402(a).

In 1962, the Truth in Negotiations Act ("TINA")[226] was enacted, which required offerors to disclose all relevant "cost or pricing" data in connection with negotiated contracts. The intent of the law was to achieve *full disclosure of facts* available to offerors so that the Government and the offeror could negotiate on an equal footing. Prior to price agreement, the offeror is required to make a written certification that the data it has provided to the Government are accurate, current and complete.[227]

Cost or pricing data means all *facts* that as of the date of the price agreement, prudent buyers and sellers would reasonably expect to affect price negotiations significantly. Cost or pricing data are factual, not judgmental and are verifiable and auditable. They do not include judgment, but they include the data forming the basis for that judgment. They include all facts that can be reasonably expected to contribute to the soundness of estimates of future costs, such as vendor quotations, nonrecurring costs, information on changes in production methods or volume, data supporting business prospects, unit cost trends, make or buy decisions, and information on management decisions that could have a significant bearing on costs.[228]

The contracting officer must obtain information adequate to determine that prices are reasonable and realistic, which means obtaining cost or pricing data. The threshold for obtaining these data are contracting actions of $550,000 or more. Unless subject to an exception, whenever any one of the following actions exceeds the threshold, cost or pricing data are required: award of any negotiated contract, the award of subcontracts where each higher-tier subcontractor and the contractor was required to furnish cost or pricing data, and any modification to any sealed bid or negotiated contract (whether or not cost or pricing data were initially required).[229] In the following situations, cost or pricing data are *not* required, and the contracting officer is *not* permitted to request or obtain it:

---

[226] 10 U.S.C. § 2306a, 41 U.S.C. § 254(d).

[227] FAR 15.406-2.

[228] 10 U.S.C. § 2306a(h)(1); 41 U.S.C. § 254b; FAR 15.401.

[229] FAR 15.403-4.

- For acquisitions at or below the simplified acquisition threshold ($100,000);[230]

- Where prices are set by law or regulation (such as utility prices);[231]

- In a contract for commercial items or modifications to a contract or subcontract for commercial items;[232]

- Where the head of a contracting agency issues a waiver in exceptional cases;[233]

- When the contracting officer determines that prices agreed upon are based on adequate price competition (i.e., two or more offerors competing independently submit priced offerors and award will be made to the proposal that represents the best value, there is no finding that the price is unreasonable; there was a reasonable expectation that two or more responsible offerors would submit offerors even though only one was received, or price analysis demonstrates that the price is reasonable for the same or similar items);[234] or

- For the exercise of an option at the price established at contract award.[235]

Contracting officers are directed not to obtain more information than is necessary in order to evaluate price reasonableness or determine cost realism. When not permitted to obtain cost or pricing information, the contracting officer may obtain other information from the offeror (i.e., information other than cost or pricing data), including prices at which the

---

[230] FAR 15.403-1(a).

[231] FAR 15.403-1(b)(2).

[232] FAR 15.403-1(b)(3).

[233] FAR 15.403-1(b)(4).

[234] FAR 15.403-1(b)(1).

[235] FAR 15.403-2.

same item or similar items have previously been sold.[236] Unlike cost or pricing data, the offeror need not certify to the accuracy, completeness and currency of the information other than cost or pricing data.

It is vitally important that a contractor provide accurate, complete and current cost or pricing data. A knowingly false certification may result in criminal or civil prosecution. Equally as important, TINA provides that if, after award, cost or pricing data are found to be inaccurate, incomplete or noncurrent as of the date of final agreement on price; the Government is entitled to a price reduction for any significant amount by which the price was increased because of the defective data.[237] This is known as "defective pricing." The Government's rights are contained in FAR 52.215-10 and FAR 52.215-11, the Price Reduction for Defective Cost or Pricing Data clauses. These clauses presume that the Government would have made the price reduction indicated by the missing data, and that the Government may now retroactively reduce the price. (The Government's proof of nondisclosure, inaccurate or noncurrent disclosure creates a rebuttable presumption that the "natural and probable consequence" of such nondisclosure was an overstated negotiated contract price.[238]) The contractor's only defenses to a Government defective pricing claim are:

1. The undisclosed data were not cost or pricing data.

2. The undisclosed data were not reasonably available.

3. The undisclosed data were actually submitted to the Government, or notice of the data were given to the Government.

4. The Government did not and would not have relied on the undisclosed data.

5. The Government cannot show that the undisclosed data caused the price to be increased.

---

[236] FAR 15.403-3.

[237] FAR 15.407-1(b)(1).

[238] *Sylvania Electric Prods., Inc. v. United States*, 202 Ct. Cl. 116, 479 F.2d 1342 (1973).

6.   The Government failed to advise the offeror about data the contracting officer knew were defective, and the Government now seeks a reduction for the same data.

The following defenses to defective pricing allegations are not likely to be successful: the contractor did not submit a certification of currency, accuracy and completeness; the contractor lost money on the contract; the contractor had inadequate time to prepare its proposal; final payment on the contract has been made; the contractor was a sole source; the contractor submitted complete data but did not tell the Government of their relevance; the contracting officer should have known the data were defective; or the contract was based on "bottom-line" price and there was no agreement about the cost of each item. Although these defenses have been tried, they usually fail.

Most defective pricing is discovered through audits performed some time after the contract is completed when all data are known and contained in the contractor's files. Every negotiated contract (except those for acquisitions below the simplified acquisition threshold of $100,000, for commercial items, or for utility services) must include the audit clause at FAR 52.215-2,[239] or a similar audit clause, which permits the Government to examine the contractor's records for up to three years after final payment under the contract.

A typical defective pricing audit might disclose the following. The contractor's accounts payable department routinely sends cost or pricing data to the negotiator on the 15th of every month. In a particular procurement, the contractor disclosed current, complete and accurate data on January 15th. This data showed that the price per pound of the significant material in the product was $10.00 (the last supplier's invoice). The Government and the contractor negotiate a contract for 400,000 end items based on this data, and agree on the price on January 25th. After the contract is completed, the auditors discover that on January 20th, the contractor received a new supplier's invoice for $9.00 per pound, but this supplier's invoice was never disclosed to the Government. The contract was defectively priced.

As a result, the auditors will find that every pound of material was defectively priced by $1.00. If there is one pound of material in each of the

---

[239] FAR 15.209(b)(1).

end items, the defective pricing totals $400,000 (400,000 items X $1 per pound), and the Government will demand a refund of that amount.

The contractor has no defense that the negotiator was unaware of the invoice, for it is the company that is negotiating the contract, and the company must ensure that its negotiator is given current, accurate and complete data.[240] The relatively simple solution for the company to ensure that the data meets the legal requirement is for the negotiator to conduct "sweeps" of the responsible offices within the company at the last possible time prior to signing the certification. The negotiator can responsibly send memos to each department involved in the procurement, asking them to confirm the most accurate, current and complete data, and providing it to the Government, before price agreement, if there has been any change since the company's last submission. TINA is a *disclosure* statute only, and as long as the data have been disclosed and their significance identified, the contractor has met all legal obligations thereunder.

H. Summary: Rules for Negotiated Procurement

1. Upon initial receipt of the RFP, examine it closely to determine whether the best value scheme is a cost/technical tradeoff or a lowest-priced, technically acceptable process, and prepare a proposal accordingly.

2. Examine Section M, the Evaluation Factors for Award of the RFP and determine the relative importance of each factor.

3. Follow the Instructions to Offerors in Section L with extreme care. Adhere to any page limits in the RFP.

4. Upon first reading the RFP, annotate every requirement in a checklist, and compare the final proposal to the checklist to ensure that every requirement has been fully and completely addressed.

5. If oral proposals are required, do practice "dry runs" to ensure that company representatives are properly prepared.

---

[240] If the negotiator knew about the January 20th invoice, but failed to disclose it, and certified that the cost or pricing data were current, accurate or complete, both the negotiator and the company have likely committed fraud.

6.   Respond to any clarification requests fully and completely.

7.   If excluded from the competitive range, seek an immediate debriefing or, if denied one by the contracting officer, consider a bid protest.

8.   Respond fully and completely to any matter brought up in oral or written discussions.

9.   When asked for proposal revisions (whether interim or final), respond fully and within the allotted time. Make changes *only* in the areas identified by the agency as deficiencies or weaknesses.

10. If not awarded a contract, request a debriefing in writing upon receipt of notification. Insist that the debriefing contain all of the elements required by the FAR.

11. If the RFP requires the submission of cost or pricing data pursuant to TINA, make certain that all required data submitted are accurate, current and complete.

12. Conduct last minute "sweeps" of all cost or pricing data just prior to price agreement and certification of the data. If new, more current data have become available, submit it to the Government in writing *prior* to executing the TINA certification.

VI. PROTESTS

For better or worse, protests have become part of the procurement process. One good aspect of having a protest mechanism is that it ensures that the procurement process is performed properly. One undesirable aspect of the protest system is that over the years it has become very easy to file a protest, especially at the General Accounting Office ("GAO"). Indeed, all it takes is a 34 cent stamp to file a protest. Although it may be that easy, it will not be that inexpensive. Filing a protest takes time and money. Thus, protesting for the sake of protesting serves no good purpose and should not be done. This section attempts to answer the questions of what are protestable issues, when does it make sense to file a protest, what protest forums are available, and what is the likelihood of winning.

A. What is Protestable—a Violation of Law or Regulation

In order to protest there must be a violation of a law or regulation. Protests are sustained or granted where an agency decision directly violates a specific law or regulation.

Protest grounds generally fall into five major categories as follows.

1.   **Improper actions in evaluation and negotiation**, including failure to follow evaluation criteria in the solicitation, failure to conduct discussions properly, and an improper cost/technical trade-off

2.   **Improper acceptance of nonconforming proposals or non-responsive bids or not awarding to conforming or responsive ones**

3.   **Improper actions involving solicitations or requirements**, such as a defect in solicitation or failure to provide bidder with material amendment to solicitation

4.   **Improper actions involving small business**, such as improper failure to set aside procurement for small business

5.   **Improper restrictions on competition**, such as improper sole source award

Although the above list is not exhaustive, it shows the types of protests that will be considered, and which have some chance of being sustained.

B. Protest Forums

There are two protest forums available to protesters—the General Accounting Office and the Court of Federal Claims. The U.S. district courts formerly had jurisdiction but that was removed. In addition, a protester always has the option of first filing a complaint with the procuring agency.

Although most protests are lodged with the GAO, the sustain rate is only about 20 percent. Fewer than 100 protest decisions are sustained by the GAO a year.

The Court of Federal Claims appears to have a higher rate of sustained protests. This does not necessarily mean that a protester should file a protest in the Court of Federal Claims in the hopes of having a higher probability of winning. The GAO is generally more knowledgeable because it hears the most bid protest cases. GAO renders decisions relatively quickly—it must issue a decision within 100 calendar days or 65 days under the express option procedures. There is no designated time for rendering a decision in the Court of Federal Claims. Finally, and, most importantly, there are different remedies available in each forum. The GAO can make recommendations to the agency but does not have the authority to direct the agency to take action. However, most of the time agencies follow the GAO's recommendation. The GAO can recommend a variety of nonmonetary remedies, such as issuing a new solicitation, terminating a contract, reopening discussions, conducting a new round of final proposals, and reevaluating proposals.[241] Protesters before the GAO may also recover the costs of pursuing the protest, including attorneys' fees and the costs of preparing the bid or proposal.[242] The Court of Federal Claims may issue a temporary restraining order or preliminary injunction or declaratory relief or permanent injunction. The monetary remedies are generally limited to the costs of preparing the bid or proposal.[243] In some cases the protester may receive attorneys' fees and expenses under the Equal Access to Justice Act.[244] Thus, choosing a forum is a strategic decision. A protester must weigh such factors as speed of decision, desired relief, and the cost of pursuing an action before selecting a forum.

---

[241] 31 U.S.C. § 3554(b)(1).

[242] 31 U.S.C. § 3554(c)(B).

[243] 28 U.S.C. § 1491(a)(1) or § 1491(b)(2).

[244] The Equal Access to Justice Act provides that prevailing individuals with a net worth of less than $2 million or prevailing firms with a net worth of less than $7 million and fewer than 500 employees may recover fees and other expenses, including reasonable attorneys' fees, unless the court finds that the position of the Government was substantially justified. 28 U.S.C. § 2412(d)(1)(A).

C. Who May Protest

In general, a prospective contractor must be an interested party or a disappointed bidder in order to protest. The term "interested party" means that the party pursuing the protest is "an actual or prospective bidder or offeror whose direct economic interest would be affected by the award of the contract or by the failure to award the contract."[245] An *actual* bidder or offeror is easy to figure out—any bidder or offeror who *actually* submits a bid or offer is an interested party. A *prospective* bidder or offeror is more problematic. If a party does not participate in a procurement nor has the capability of participating in the procurement, then the party will not be a prospective bidder or offeror. Also, if a party knowingly removes itself from the bidding, it will not be considered a prospective bidder.[246] On the other hand, if a party would have submitted an offer but did not because the specifications were defective, it will be considered a prospective bidder or offeror.

To be an interested party, an actual or prospective bidder or offeror must also have a direct economic interest in the procurement. This means that an actual or prospective bidder or offeror must be in line for award or be able to compete for award if its position in the protest is upheld. This is easy to determine in sealed bidding. The second low bidder has a direct economic interest in a procurement, whereas the third low bidder—as well as lower ranked bidders—do not. In negotiated procurement it is much harder to determine whether a protester has a direct economic interest in the award. Several factors must be considered, such as the nature of the issue raised, the relief sought, and the party's status in relation to the procurement.[247] For example, a party will be deemed to have a direct economic interest if the relief being requested is to permit all of the offerors to submit revised proposals. A party will also be found to have a direct economic interest if it claims that its proposal was improperly evaluated and that proper evaluation would have put it in line for award.[248]

---

[245] 31 U.S.C. § 3551(2).

[246] *Federal Data Corp. v. United States*, 911 F.2d 699 (Fed. Cir. 1990).

[247] *Meridian Management Corp.*, Comp. Gen. Dec. B-271557, 96-2 CPD ¶ 64.

[248] *See, e.g., Northwest EnviroService, Inc.*, 71 Comp. Gen. 453 (B-247380.2), 92-2 CPD ¶ 38 (protester argued that had its past performance

D. Time for Protesting at the GAO

1. Time Limitations

There are strict time limitations on filing a protest at the GAO,[249] and any contractor that seeks to file should move very quickly:

- **Improprieties in solicitation that are apparent *prior* to bid opening or the closing date for receipt of proposals**—protest must be filed prior to bid opening or the closing date for receipt of proposals.[250]

- **All other cases**—protest must be filed not later than 10 days after the basis of the protest is known or should have been known, whichever is earlier.[251]

There is an exception for protests challenging a negotiated procurement where a debriefing is requested, and, when requested, is required. In such case, with respect to any protest basis that is known or should have been known either before or as a result of the debriefing—the initial protest cannot be filed before the debriefing date offered to the protester but must be filed not later than 10 calendar days[252] after the date on which the debriefing is held.[253] The Comptroller General will not consider a protest challenging a

---

been properly evaluated it would have been the best value because it offered the lowest cost); and *Rome Research Corp.*, Comp. Gen. Dec. B-245797.4, 92-2 CPD ¶ 194 (protester asserted that had its management and technical qualifications been properly evaluated it would have been the best value because it was the lowest cost offeror).

[249] The courts have no set time limits for filing a protest.

[250] 4 C.F.R. § 21.2(a)(1).

[251] 4 C.F.R. § 21.2(a)(2).

[252] 4 C.F.R. § 21.0(e) states that in computing any period of time, "the day from which the period begins to run is not counted, and when the last day of the period is a Saturday, Sunday, or Federal holiday, the period extends to the next day that is not a Saturday, Sunday, or Federal holiday."

[253] 4 C.F.R. § 21.2(a)(2).

negotiated procurement in which a debriefing is requested and required if filed before the debriefing date offered to the protester.[254]

2. *Statutory Stay at the GAO (Suspension of Award or Contract Performance)*

In order to ensure that effective relief may be obtained by successful protesters, the statutes for protests before the GAO contain provisions that delay award or suspend contract performance pending the decision on a protest. This is known as the "statutory stay" or the "CICA stay" because it is mandated by the Competition in Contracting Act. These rules are as follows:

- **If a protest is filed before award**—a contract may not be awarded.[255]

- **If a protest is filed within 10 calendar days after contract award or 5 calendar days after a debriefing**—the agency must suspend contract performance.[256]

An agency is required to suspend performance only if it receives notice from the GAO within 10 days of contract award. Thus, if a protester wants to ensure that contract performance is suspended, it should submit its protest to the GAO by the ninth day of the period, thereby leaving sufficient time for GAO to notify the agency.

The time periods for filing a protest and the statutory stay at the GAO should be reviewed together. A protester could find itself in the position of meeting the time period for filing a protest but not meeting the time restrictions for obtaining a statutory stay. For example:

February 1st	Contract award
February 5th	Date of debriefing
February 10th	Offeror A files protest at GAO

---

[254] *Real Estate Ctr.*, Comp. Gen. Dec. B-274081, 96-2 CPD ¶ 74.

[255] 31 U.S.C. § 3553(c).

[256] 31 U.S.C. § 3553.

| February 13th | Offeror B files protest at GAO |
| February 17th | Offeror C files protest at GAO |

Offeror	Timeliness/Stay
Offeror A	Protest timely filed and agency must suspend contract award
Offeror B	Protest timely filed but agency does not have to suspend contract award
Offeror C	Protest is not timely filed and will be dismissed

There is no automatic statutory stay for protests filed at either a U.S. district court or the Court of Federal Claims. For protests filed in those forums the protester has the option of seeking a temporary restraining order or preliminary injunction.[257]

3.   CICA Override of Stay at GAO

Even if a protester files in a timely manner to get the statutory stay at the GAO, an agency may override the stay on the basis of urgent and compelling circumstances or, in the case of postaward protests, on a finding of urgent and compelling circumstances or if the override is in the Government's best interests.[258] This is called the "CICA Override." Usually an override is approved of at the head of contracting activity level. A protester may contest the CICA override by filing in a U.S. district court. Thus, even through the protest is filed at the GAO, the protester will be required to bring an action in U.S. district court if it elects to contest the CICA override.

---

[257] 28 U.S.C. § 1491(b)(2). *See* Rule 65(b) (TROs) and Rule 65(a) (preliminary injunction) of the Federal Rules of Civil Procedure for rules on issuing such orders.

[258] 31 U.S.C. § 3553(c)(2) and (d)(3)(C).

E. Determining Whether to Protest

Just because there is a protestable issue does not necessarily mean a company should protest. There are a lot of questions that need to be asked, such as:

- **Does the agency have a lot of discretion on the contestable issue**. For instance, a company may believe that the agency gave it a lower past performance score than it deserved. The agency has a lot of discretion in this area and chances are the company will not win on this issue alone. This does not mean that a company will never win on a dispute about past performance. It just means that if everything else in the procurement looks proper, it is unlikely that the Comptroller General or a court will sustain a protest on this basis.

- **Does the company have the money to spend on a protest**. Filing a protest takes money. There is no filing fee at the GAO. However, the filing fee at the Court of Federal Claims is $120. That is the inexpensive part. A simple protest at the GAO can cost about $3,000. A complex protest can cost much more. The complete prosecution of the protest before the GAO can cost from about $8,000 to $40,000 (or more) depending on the complexity of the case. A protester in a U.S. district court or the Court of Federal Claims may also have to incur the significant costs of depositions and interrogatories.

- **Can the company better spend its time and resources bidding on another solicitation, especially if the likelihood of actually winning is small**. A company must realize that defending a protest takes resources and time—resources that could be put to other tasks.

- **How valid is the protest versus how is protesting going to impact the company's currently good working relationship with the agency**. A company should ask itself whether it is willing to jeopardize its working relationship over a protestable issue. Good working relationships take a long time to establish. This does not mean that a company should be intimidated from ever protesting for fear of repercussions. Contracting officials are professionals and are expected to act in a professional manner toward all contractors, including those that have protested in the past.

F. Protest Depositions and Discovery

Discovery in all forums (courts and the GAO) is limited. Both in the courts and GAO, the agency must produce the relevant documents. However, only with the court's or GAO's permission may parties take depositions (i.e., asking questions of the other party or a witness, under oath), submit written questions, or obtain additional documents beyond the agency record. The most common method of discovery in protests before the GAO is the production of documents. Every GAO protest should include a request for documents. Documents requested should include all documents which formed the agency's award decision.

G. Form and Content of Protest

Protests must be in writing. Protests must be filed directly with the GAO—if it is a GAO protest or the court—if it is a protest before the Court of Federal Claims. A copy of the protest should be sent to the contracting officer. Court filing requirements are contained in the Court rules. At the GAO, a protest may be hand delivered or sent by mail, commercial carrier, or facsimile. If a protest is sent by facsimile, it is important to confirm that the GAO received the protest. The protester, or its attorney, should call the GAO and verify that the protest was received. Also, the protester should keep the facsimile printout stating that the transmission was received.

Protests at the GAO must include the following information:

- Name, address, email, and fax and telephone numbers of the protester

- Signature of the protester or its representative

- Solicitation or contract number and name of the contracting agency

- Detailed statement of the legal and factual grounds for the protest, to include a description of resulting prejudice to the protester

- Copies of relevant documents

- Request for a ruling by the GAO

- Statement as to the form of relief requested

- Statement that the protester seeks a CICA stay (if appropriate)

- All information establishing that the protester is an interested party for the purpose of filing a protest

- All information establishing the timeliness of a protest

- Request specific documents, a protective order or a hearing (optional)[259]

An unsuccessful offeror should ensure that it completed everything specified in the above list before actually filing a protest.

H. What Protests Are More likely to Win

The most likely protests to win are those that involve very straightforward issues, such as (1) an agency's failure to make award to a responsive low bid, or an agency's improper award to a nonresponsive low bid; (2) an agency's improper conduct of discussions (e.g., conducting discussions with one offeror in the competitive range, but failing to conduct discussions with all offerors in the competitive range); (3) outright failure of the agency to apply the evaluation factors stated in the RFP (e.g., the agency uses a completely different evaluation scheme than what it identified in the solicitation); and (4) agency failure to properly apply socioeconomic provisions (such as price differential).

It is much more difficult to win a protest involving the interpretation of the regulations or the appropriateness of the agency's scoring. For example, it is extremely difficult to convince either the GAO or a court that an agency improperly scored a proposal (such as arguing that a score of 75 out of 100 should have been scored as 85) because both the court and the GAO are extremely deferential to the agency's decisions and will only disturb them if

---

[259] 4 C.F.R. § 21.1(c).

they are irrational, arbitrary and capricious. Similarly, disagreements over interpretations of an RFP usually are not winning protests.

I. What does Winning Mean

Winning a protest seldom means that the GAO or court is going to recommend that the agency direct award to the protester. More often, it simply means that the protester will be back in the game. For instance, in a protest before the GAO, the GAO may sustain a protest on the basis that the agency should have conducted discussions. In such a case, the GAO will probably recommend that the agency go back and conduct proper discussions and then reevaluate the proposals. In another example, if it is determined that a protester was improperly eliminated from the competitive range, a likely recommendation will be to include the protester in the competitive range and reevaluate proposals.

J. Appeals

The Court of Federal Claims decisions may be appealed to the Court of Appeals for the Federal Circuit. Since the GAO is an administrative forum that is part of the legislative branch of the Government, there is no appeal to any court. Rather, if a protester loses a protest before the GAO, it can bring a suit before the Court of Federal Claims or district court, if time permits. Agency reports filed with the Comptroller General are to be considered as part of the agency record in the court hearing. The court will not make a de novo (new) review but, rather, will determine whether the Comptroller General's recommendation was rational.[260] There is some disagreement as to whether a Comptroller General's decision should be given deference. Some courts believe that the Comptroller General's decision should be given great deference.[261] The Court of Appeals for the District of Columbia believes that the Comptroller General's decision should be regarded as expert opinion to

---

[260] *Honeywell, Inc. v. United States*, 870 F.2d 644 (Fed. Cir. 1989).

[261] *See, e.g., Carothers Constr., Inc. v. United States*, 18 Cl. Ct. 745 (1989); *Qualmed, Inc. v. Office of Civilian Health & Med. Program of the Armed Servs.*, 934 F. Supp. 1227 (D. Col. 1996); and *Halifax Technical Servs., Inc v. United States*, 848 F. Supp. 240 (D.D.C. 1994).

which it should consider but to which it has no obligation to defer.[262] In bid protest matters, the Court of Federal Claims gives deference to the Comptroller General, but must answer the question of whether the agency's procurement decision or the GAO's decision on the protest was reasonable based on the record before the contracting officer or Comptroller General.[263]

K. Summary: Rules for Protests

1. Carefully weigh the merits and weaknesses of protesting before filing a protest.

2. Ensure that the protest explains why it is timely, that the protester is an interested party, and asks for specific relief.

3. File preaward solicitation protest issues prior to contract award.

4. File postaward protest issues within 10 days after the basis of the protest is known.

5. Seek a statutory stay of contract performance at the GAO by protesting within the specified time frames; this places pressure on the agency to settle.

---

[262] *See Delta Data Systems Corp. v. Webster*, 744 F.2d 197 (D.C. Cir. 1984).

[263] *E.W. Bliss Co. v. United States*, 33 Fed. Cl. 123 (1995); *Cubic Applications v. United States*, 37 Fed. Cl. 339 (1997).

CHAPTER 3

SOCIOECONOMIC POLICIES AND PROGRAMS

The Government uses the acquisition process to implement a wide variety of socioeconomic policies that are considered to be in the national interest. These include: assistance to small businesses in order to help them grow and to provide "seeds" for future large businesses, direct award (without competition) to certain small and disadvantaged businesses, preferences for small businesses in historically underutilized business zones, domestic preferences for articles made in America or made in certain specific qualifying countries, policies favoring the environment and equal employment opportunity, enforcing minimum wage laws, and a requirement for a drug-free work place. These policies work in conjunction with the procurement methods described in this book, sometimes conflicting with stated policies in contract formation. For example, a procurement that is set-aside for small business is not conducted using "full and open" competition and might result in a higher price than a procurement open to all sources; however, the policy is to accept such a higher price in order to "favor" small businesses where appropriate and within the statutory guidelines.

I. POLICIES AND PREFERENCES

A. Policies and Programs to Assist Small Businesses

There are a number of programs designed to assist small businesses in the procurement process. The programs are under the control and supervision of the Small Business Administration ("SBA"). The SBA establishes size standards, rules on size appeals, and is solely authorized to make determinations that a small business is not a responsible contractor. One form of preference is through "set-aside." This preference authorizes procuring agencies to set-aside procurements (total set-aside) or portions of procurements (partial set-aside) for the exclusive participation of small business concerns, as long as prices are reasonable.[264]

---

[264] 15 U.S.C. § 644.

B. Small Business Concern

A small business concern is independently owned and operated and not dominant in its field of operation. The definition of small business varies by industry. To qualify, a contractor must fall within the size standard applicable to the industry under the North American Industry Classification System ("NAICS").[265] Depending on the industry in question, the standard applied is based on either dollar volume or number of employees.[266]

C. Small Disadvantaged Businesses

A small disadvantaged business concern is a small business concern that is at least 51 percent unconditionally owned by one or more individuals who are both socially and economically disadvantaged; or a publicly owned business with at least 51 percent of its stock unconditionally owned by, and its management and daily business controlled by, one or more socially and economically disadvantaged individuals.[267]

D. Small Disadvantaged Businesses—the 8(a) Program

The primary program designed to assist small disadvantaged businesses is the "8(a) program," known for the section of the Small Business Act which authorized it. This program authorizes the SBA to enter into contracts with other federal agencies and to perform such contracts by subcontracting to small businesses.[268] The SBA's subcontractors, which must be small disadvantaged business concerns, are referred to as "8(a) contractors."

E. HUBZone Empowerment Program

The HUBZone Empowerment Program is designed to provide federal contracting opportunities for certain qualified small business concerns

---

[265] *See* http://www.census.gov/epcd/www/naics.html.

[266] *See* 13 C.F.R. Part 121.

[267] 13 C.F.R. § 124.1002.

[268] 15 U.S.C. § 637(a).

located in distressed communities. The program is intended to promote private-sector investment and employment opportunities in these communities. A concern may be determined to be a qualified HUBZone small business concern if it is located in an historically underutilized business zone, is owned and controlled by one or more U.S. citizens, and at least 35 percent of its employees reside in a HUB Zone.

F. Policies for Assisting Women-Owned Enterprises

The Federal Acquisition Streamlining Act of 1994[269] amended the Small Business Act to establish a Government-wide goal for participation by women-owned and controlled small business concerns in prime contracts and subcontracts of not less than 5 percent of the total value of all prime contract and subcontract awards for each fiscal year.[270]

G. Domestic Preference Policies

There are several policies favoring the acquisition of articles of domestic origin or acquisition from a domestic source. The most prevalent are the Buy American Act[271] and the Trade Agreements Act of 1979.[272] The Buy American Act establishes a general preference for the acquisition of domestic "articles, materials, and supplies" when they are being acquired for public use in the United States. The Buy American Act provision[273] is required to be included in solicitations for supply contracts. It requires the offeror to certify that each end product, other than those specifically identified in the certificate, is of domestic origin, and that components of unknown origin have been considered to have been mined, produced, or manufactured outside the United States. Implementation of the Buy American Act is contained in FAR Subpart 25.1. Another significant program giving preference to American products over foreign products is the Balance of Payments Program. This program applies to acquisitions of work to be performed outside the United States. It is covered in FAR Subpart 25.3. The

---

[269] Pub. L. No. 103-355.

[270] 15 U.S.C. § 644(g).

[271] 41 U.S.C. §§ 10 a–d.

[272] 19 U.S.C. §§ 2501–2582, as amended.

[273] FAR 52.225-1.

Trade Agreements Act establishes a threshold (currently $175,000 for supply and service contracts and $6,725,000 for construction contracts), above which neither the Buy American Act nor the Balance of Payments Program restrictions applies.[274] Instead, the Government may buy a product from any "designated country," which includes many European, and some Asian and African countries. This is covered in FAR Subpart 25.4.

H. Equal Employment Opportunity

The Equal Opportunity Clause[275] is mandatory in all Government contracts exceeding $10,000.[276] The clause is also mandatory for all contracts under $10,000 if the contractor has, or reasonably can expect to have, contracts or subcontracts with the Government exceeding $10,000 in a 12-month period.[277] Under the clause, the contractor agrees not to discriminate against any employee or applicant for employment because of race, color, religion, sex, or national origin. Sanctions include cancellation of the contract and debarment of the contractor from eligibility for future Government contracts.

I. Summary Rules for Policies and Preferences

1. When submitting an offer on a procurement that is set-aside for small business, be sure to meet the SBA size standards.

2. If qualifying as an 8(a) or HUBZONE contractor, seek business opportunities through relevant agencies and the SBA.

3. Comply with the Equal Opportunity clause by not discriminating against any employee or applicant for employment because of race, color, religion, sex, or national origin.

---

[274] FAR 25.402.

[275] FAR 52.222-26.

[276] Executive Order No. 11246; FAR 22.810(e).

[277] FAR 22.807(b)(1).

4.   Ensure that end products are of domestic origin before certifying under the Buy American Act, or ensure that products come from a "designated country" if the Trade Agreements Act applies.

II. FAIR LABOR STANDARDS

The statutes covering labor standards impose minimum wage levels, overtime wage restrictions, and provisions governing working conditions on various classes of work. The principle labor standard statutes are discussed below.

A. Davis-Bacon Act

The Davis-Bacon Act[278] establishes minimum wages, including fringe benefits, to be paid to *laborers and mechanics* on contracts over $2,000 for the construction, alteration, or repair of public buildings and public works. Subcontractor employees are also covered.[279] Department of Labor regulations implementing this statute are at 29 C.F.R. Part 1. The FAR regulations are at FAR Subpart 22.4.

B. Service Contract Act

The Service Contract Act[280] Act establishes minimum wage rates and fringe benefits based on those prevailing in the locality to be paid *service employees* for contracts over $2,500 which are principally for services and are furnished by service employees.[281] Subcontractor employees are also covered.[282] The FAR regulations are at Subpart 22.10.

---

[278] 40 U.S.C. § 3141.

[279] FAR 52.222-6(a).

[280] 41 U.S.C. §§ 351-58.

[281] 41 U.S.C. § 351(a)(1).

[282] FAR 52.222-41(c).

C. Contract Work Hours and Safety Standards Act

The Contract Work Hours and Safety Standards Act[283] requires that certain contracts contain a clause specifying that no *laborer or mechanic* doing any part of the work contemplated by the contract shall be required or permitted to work more than 40 hours in any workweek unless paid for all such overtime hours at not less than one and one-half times the basic rate of pay.[284]

D. Walsh-Healey Act

The Walsh-Healey Act[285] is the *supply* contract counterpart to the Davis-Bacon Act. It establishes minimum wages for contracts in excess of $10,000 for the manufacturing or furnishing of supplies, articles and equipment. The protections of this Act have been superseded by the Fair Labor Standards Act.

E. Summary Rules for Fair Labor Practices

1.   Comply with all minimum wage and overtime wage requirements in your prime contract.

2.   Always "flow down" minimum wage requirements to all subcontracts, and monitor subcontractor performance.

III. POLICIES RELATING TO WORKPLACE AND ENVIRONMENT

A. Policies on the Environment and Energy

Congress has passed a number of statutes concerning the environment and energy. Some of the more significant statutes include the National

---

[283] 40 U.S.C. §§ 3701-3705.

[284] FAR 22.301.

[285] 41 U.S.C. § 35 *et seq.*

Environmental Policy Act,[286] the Energy Policy and Conservation Act,[287] the Noise Control Act of 1972,[288] the Resource Conservation and Energy Act of 1976,[289] the Clean Air Amendments of 1970[290] and the Water Pollution Control Act Amendments of 1972.[291]

B. Americans with Disabilities Act

The Americans with Disability Act prohibits all employers from discriminating against any "qualified individual" with a disability because of that persons disability. The remedies available to a successful complaint include hiring, reinstatement, promotion, back or front pay, reasonable accommodation, attorneys' fees, expert witness fees, and court costs.[292] In addition, compensatory and punitive damages may be available where intentional discrimination is found.[293]

C. Drug-Free Workplace Act of 1988

The Drug-Free Workplace Act of 1988[294] requires Government contractors to establish and maintain a drug-free workplace as a condition of their current contracts and in order to maintain eligibility for future contracts. The Act is implemented by FAR Subpart 23.5.

---

[286] 42 U.S.C. § 4332.

[287] Pub. L. No. 94-163, codified at 42 U.S.C. § 6361(a)(1).

[288] Pub. L. No. 92-574, codified at 42 U.S.C. § 4901 *et seq.*

[289] Pub. L. No. 94-580, codified at 42 U.S.C. § 6901 *et seq.*

[290] Pub. L. No. 91-604, codified at 42 U.S.C. § 7401 *et seq.*

[291] Pub. L. No. 92-500, codified at 33 U.S.C. § 1251 *et seq.*

[292] 42 U.S.C. § 1981a(a).

[293] *Id.*

[294] 41 U.S.C. § 701 *et seq.*

D. Summary: Rules for Policies Relating to the Workplace and Environment

1. Do not discriminate against any qualified individual with a disability because of that person's disability.

2. Establish and maintain a drug-free workplace.

CHAPTER 4

ADMINISTRATION OF GOVERNMENT CONTRACTS

I. ADMINISTRATION BASICS

A. Signed Copy of Contract Award

Not beginning contract performance until a signed copy of the contract award is in hand seems only logical. But snags frequently occur in getting the required Government signature, and the contract start date may indeed arrive before the contractor has the signed instrument. The contractor may have received a written letter outlining the Government's "intent" to award the contract, but *that is not a contract award.* Similarly, the Government frequently awards "unfunded" contracts, which contain a clause stating that the Government has no legal liability for any payment until funds are available and the contractor is so notified in writing.[295] *A contractor should not succumb to Government entreaties to begin work anyway.* Contractor costs and liability are too great, and simply stated, without a signed contract, the Government's liabilities are generally zero. This problem is magnified when the contractor is the incumbent for a follow-on contract, either in the form of a new contract or the exercise of an option. Should the contractor suspend work while waiting for the new contract, the signed exercise of an option, or the new funding? Wouldn't such a suspension be disruptive to the Government and the contractor workforce? The answer to both questions is an emphatic *yes*, but that should not sway the contractor. Even if suspension of performance would be disruptive, the contractor should avoid at all cost being in the position of providing goods and services to the Government

---

[295] FAR 52.232-18. The clause reads, in full, as follows:

> Funds are not presently available for this contract. The Government's obligation under this contract is contingent upon the availability of appropriated funds from which payment for contract purposes can be made. No legal liability on the part of the Government for any payment may arise until funds are made available to the Contracting Officer for this contract and until the Contractor receives notice of such availability, to be confirmed in writing by the Contracting Officer.

when no contractual obligations exist between the parties, or when the Government has no obligation to pay the contractor.

Similarly, no contractor should begin work if its contract or any Government correspondence states that funding for the contract is not presently available. Until the contractor receives written assurance that funds are available, it is unlikely to be paid for any work.

1. Complete Copy of Contract

It is also very important that, from the very beginning through the close-out or termination of any contract, the contractor keep a complete and accurate copy of the contract in one central place. This copy should contain every modification, every letter exercising an option, internal working papers and analyses, and all correspondence between the parties. In addition, where it is necessary to memorialize contractor actions, the file should contain written, dated, and signed "Memoranda for the File" which state the basis of contractor performance. Note, however, that unless the contractor provides the Government with copies of such file memoranda (see below), the contractor will not be able to assert with certainty that the Government knew of these interpretations of the contract.

2. Complete Copy of Solicitation Documents

As important as a complete copy of the contract is a complete copy of the solicitation—either the invitation for bids or the request for proposals, amendments, proposals, bids, abstracts, and any other written documentation pertaining to the solicitation. Of course, in many cases the contract may have been created by extracting certain portions of the solicitation (including contractor prices in the bid schedule), and superimposing a signed cover sheet such as Standard Form ("SF") 26[296] or SF 33.[297] In that case the contractor will need to copy everything so that both the contract file and the solicitation file remain complete and intact.

---

[296] FAR 53.301-26.

[297] FAR 53.301-33.

3. Files in Logical Sequence

Most contract administrators maintain their contract and solicitation files by keeping documents in reverse chronological order. In addition to filing amendments of solicitations or modifications of contracts, they usually place a "pen and ink" change on the basic contract or solicitation referring the reader to the latest change, which is filed separately by date. Besides official Government documents, the contractor should maintain copies of all contract-related correspondence between the Government and the contractor.

4. Documentation of Conversations

A key to resolving any dispute that may arise during performance of a Government contract is the careful documentation of conversations with the contracting officer or any representative of the contracting officer. Because the contractor's subsequent success in winning disputes depends in large part upon its ability to prove mutual understanding between the parties, the written record is extremely important. Even if verbal agreement has been reached, therefore, the contractor should always put its interpretation in writing, normally in the form of a letter to the contracting officer, and obtain acknowledgment of receipt of the letter. Merely informing the contracting officer in writing of an interpretation, however, does not ensure that the contracting officer concurs with that interpretation. One of the contractor's primary objectives is to obtain the contracting officer's concurrence in any given interpretation so that the matter is not disputed later. Written concurrence will resolve the issue. For an example of a routine piece of contract correspondence, see **Figure 4-1**.

B. Government Authority

As discussed previously, every contractor must understand the authority of Government officials to enter into and direct contract performance. Contracts may be entered into and signed on behalf of the Government only by contracting officers.[298] In addition, contracting officers may administer and terminate contracts, but may bind the Government only to the extent of the authority delegated to them.[299]

---

[298] FAR 1.601(a).

[299] FAR 1.602-1(a).

**LETTER TO CONTRACTING OFFICER DOCUMENTING
PROPOSED PERFORMANCE AND REQUESTING CONCURRENCE**

ABC Company
Address

Date

Ms. Jane Doe
Contracting Officer
Address

RE: Contract No. XYZ-123

Dear Ms. Doe:

The ABC company is replacing washers and dryers at your facility pursuant to Contract XYZ-123, which requires the former contractor to pick up the old machines. Despite seven different telephone calls by us, as well as several phone calls by your contract specialist, we have been unable to reach the former contractor to make firm arrangements for pickup. Therefore, as we install new machines, if the former contractor is not on hand to receive each machine as it is replaced, we shall place each old machine in the corner of the room, disconnected and ready for pickup. The new machines will be operable.

Please indicate your agreement with this direction by signing below where indicated and mailing or faxing this letter back to us.

Very truly yours,

John Smith
Contractor

Concur: _____
        Contracting Officer

Date: _____

Figure 4-1

When given the responsibility of administering the contract, an Administrative Contracting Officer may perform routine administrative functions such as reviewing progress payment requests, monitoring labor relations, performing engineering analyses of cost proposals, and ensuring compliance with contractual quality assurance and safety requirements.[300] However, unless specifically authorized by the PCO, the ACO may *not* negotiate or issue change orders; neither can the ACO change the contract price, specifications (configuration of items or services), delivery schedule, or quantity.[301]

Although the CORs, COTRs, inspectors, ACOs, auditors, and contract specialists serve as the "eyes and ears" of the contracting officer,[302] they are not the "mouth" of the contracting officer. *The only Government official with authority to change price, delivery schedule, specifications, or quantity is the contracting officer.* Negotiations with anyone but the contracting officer are not binding on the Government unless that particular member of the team has been delegated the responsibility to make the decision—and that is the exception rather than the rule. For example, a contractor should never rely on a contract specialist's statement that a particular delay is acceptable to the Government. *The statement of a contract specialist does not bind the Government because it is the contracting officer, not the contract specialist, who has the authority to do so.* **Figure 4-2** shows those officials who legally possess authority to negotiate, award and make changes to a contract. Only those officials in the dark boxes possess such legal authority.

If the contractor disagrees with anyone on the contracting officer's team on a particular issue, the contractor should *raise the issue in writing with the contracting officer and obtain the contracting officer's written decision or advice.* The contractor should not rely on any written or oral commitment from a person other than the contracting officer concerning anything significant. A careful contractor will ensure that all significant correspondence goes to the contracting officer and that it in turn receives the contracting officer's assent to any change that might affect price, delivery schedule, quantity, or specifications. Etiquette calls for addressing correspondence to the contracting officer, further addressed (or copied) to the attention of the

---

[300] FAR 42.302(a).

[301] FAR 42.302(b).

[302] *Precision Products*, ASBCA No. 25280, 82-2 BCA ¶ 15,981.

ACO, inspector, contract specialist, or other specialist with whom the contractor has had contact. See **Figure 4-3**.

CONTRACTING AUTHORITY

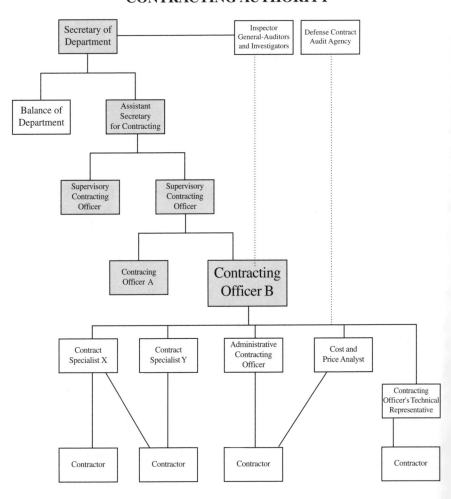

Figure 4.2

LETTER TO CONTRACTING OFFICER REQUESTING
CONFIRMATION OF CONTRACT SPECIALIST'S INTERPRETATION

ABC Company
Address

April 29, 1994

Ms. Jane Doe
Contracting Officer
Address

RE: Contract No. XYZ-123

Dear Ms. Doe:

　　　　Yesterday, Ms. Karen Smith, contract specialist, advised the undersigned that the Government had agreed to accept a 30-day delay in the delivery of 200 blue summer uniforms that are contractually due on May 1, 1994. Ms. Smith advised that the Government acknowledged that it had failed to select the exact color in time for the contractually required delivery, and therefore was extending the delivery date, with no change in price.

　　　　Please sign below and fax a copy of this letter to me to indicate your concurrence.

Very truly yours,

John Smith
Contractor

cc: Karen Smith, contract specialist

Concur

_____

Jane Doe, Contracting Officer

Figure 4-3

C. Interpreting Contract Requirements

After contract award, there may be disagreement between the contractor and the Government over the proper interpretation of the instrument itself.

The fundamental principle used by the courts is that the contract will be read as a whole—all aspects of the contract will be interpreted together.[303] This means that reasonable meaning must be assigned to all parts of the contract, with none rendered meaningless.[304]

Simply stated, the contract must be read so as to fulfill the principal purposes intended by the parties when entering into the contract; those provisions that could be interpreted as being either in conflict or in harmony should be interpreted as being in harmony. In some cases, evidence outside the contract, such as facts ascertained when the contract was formed or during earlier performance, are used to assist in resolving contract interpretation controversies. Examples include discussions and requests for clarifications prior to submission of bids or offers, statements made in prebid or preproposal conferences, prior course of dealing between the parties, and standard trade usage.

Finally, even when an offeror submits a detailed proposal in response to a solicitation, the Government is generally considered to be the *drafter* of the contract that will be formed. This is important, because when contracts cannot be satisfactorily interpreted according to the rules above, they will be interpreted against the drafter (the Government) or, in legal terms, *contra proferentem*.[305] This approach places liability for ambiguity on the Government, the party that could have prevented the controversy by using clearer language.[306] However, contractors may not later take advantage of vagueness previously known to them; contractors have a duty to seek clarification of any obvious ambiguity *before* submitting a bid or offer in order to avoid postaward disputes.[307] This duty also serves contractors well by providing an incentive to know and understand their responsibilities before being legally bound.

---

[303] *Restatement (Second) of Contracts* § 202(2).

[304] *Fortec Constructors v. United States*, 760 F.2d 1288, 1292 (Fed. Cir. 1985).

[305] *Restatement (Second) of Contracts* § 206.

[306] *Sturm v. United States*, 190 Ct. Cl. 691 (1970).

[307] *S.O.G. of Ark. v. United States*, 212 Ct. Cl. 125, 131 (1976).

D. Design and Performance Specifications

When the Government provides the specifications to be used in performing the work, it is responsible for the adequacy of those specifications. This is known as the "implied warranty of specifications."[308] When the Government supplies "design specifications" that set forth the exact manner, materials, and method in which the contractor is expected to perform, and the specifications do not work, the Government is responsible for the failure. Blueprints or detailed drawings in a solicitation are examples of design specifications. When using design specifications, the Government frequently provides blueprints or detailed drawings, and requires the contractor to follow them.

When the Government supplies only "performance specifications," which set forth an objective end result without specifying exactly how to achieve it, the contractor may select the means of accomplishing the work, and there is no warranty of specifications.[309] An example of a simple performance specification is: "furnish a washing machine that can wash 10 pounds of clothing in 30 minutes or less."

If the design specifications are defective, the contractor is entitled to recover from the Government any increased costs caused by the defects. For example, if specified materials do not work as intended in the contract, or if required dimensions make the end product unusable, the contractor has a valid claim for the additional costs of producing the intended item or making the end product usable. Any time specifications are found to be defective, the contractor should immediately alert the contracting officer in writing, thereby providing the notice for any potential equitable adjustment or claim under the contract.

E. Cooperation Between the Parties

Every contract imposes on both the contractor and the Government a duty of good faith and fair dealing in the performance and enforcement of the contract.[310] The contractor must attempt to assist the Government when

---

[308] *United States v. Spearin*, 248 U.S. 132 (1918).

[309] *Big Chief Drilling Co. v. United States*, 26 Cl. Ct. 1276, 1294 (1992).

[310] *Restatement (Second) of Contracts* § 205.

problems arise, even if this results in change orders. The Government must make a good-faith effort not to hinder the contractor (with overzealous inspection, for example) and must work with the contractor to solve unanticipated problems. Other examples where the contractor may have a valid claim against the Government include the Government's failure to: issue a timely notice to proceed, respond to a contractor's request to perform inspections, respond to requests for information, deliver Government-furnished property in a timely fashion, and assist the contractor in solving problems that arise during contract performance.

F. Summary: Rules for Principles of Contract Administration

1. Do not start to perform the contract before receiving a signed copy of the contract award.

2. Do not start to perform before receiving written notice that funds are available.

3. Maintain a complete copy of the contract in a central place.

4. Maintain a complete copy of the solicitation and the bid or proposal.

5. Maintain all contract files in reverse chronological sequence.

6. Comply fully with every contract as written and awarded, unless a change order from a warranted contracting officer is issued.

7. Document all conversations with a contracting officer or his or her representative.

8. Maintain a complete and current copy of all regulations that apply to the contract.

9. Establish company ethics codes and compliance programs.

10. Take direction only from Government Officials with actual authority (primarily the contracting officer), and have all direction confirmed in writing.

11. Read and interpret the requirements of the contract as a whole.

12. Follow design specifications exactly and immediately advise the contracting officer if they are defective.

13. Cooperate with the Government in the performance of the contract (remembering that the Government, too, is required to cooperate).

II. DAY-TO-DAY CONTRACT ADMINISTRATION

This section discusses routine matters that occur on a regular basis in the administration of Government contracts. They concern bread and butter items that will recur over and over, when a contract is being performed smoothly and without problems.

A. Records Management

All Government contractors should maintain adequate record keeping systems. This is especially true where the contract contains one of the audit clauses that grant the Government the right to examine contractor books.[311] It is possible to avoid audits by bidding only on fixed-price contracts pursuant to sealed-bid procurements, where no cost or pricing data[312] is required or submitted pursuant to the Truth In Negotiations Act.[313] Most Government contractors, however, are subject at one time or another to an audit, and a solid records management program is therefore needed. "Records" include data of any kind, which could be on paper, computer, audio or video cassette, etc.

A good records management program includes three key elements: (1) written guidance outlining policy and procedures; (2) retention of records for the prescribed period; and (3) destruction of records at the end of the

---

[311] FAR 52.214-26, Audit and Records—Sealed Bidding; FAR 52.215-2, Audit and Records—Negotiations; and FAR 52.212-5(d),Contract Terms and Conditions Required to Implement Statutes or Executive Orders—Commercial Items (audit provisions for commercial items).

[312] FAR 15.403.

[313] 10 U.S.C. § 2306a; 41 U.S.C. § 2548.

prescribed period unless the records are the subject of an audit, investigation (subpoena or other legitimate request), or are otherwise needed in the course of business.

The FAR prescribes the required period for retention of records as follows:

- Financial and cost accounting records: four years, except labor cost distribution cards (two years) and petty cash records (two years).

- Pay administration records: four years for payroll sheets, registers, and tax withholding statements; two years for clock cards and paid checks, receipts for wages paid in cash, or other payments for services rendered by employees.

- Acquisition and supply records: four years for everything except requisitions (two years).[314]

Contractors should have written policies supporting the proper retention period and a systematic method of certifying destroyed records at the end of the period, including the purging of computer drives. Records destruction is just as important as records retention not only because it eliminates the cost and burden of storage, but also because it permits the contractor to respond to any audit or investigation request *after* the retention period with a certificate of destruction, rather than the records. Remember to destroy all computer records and disks in addition to hard copies.

B. First Article Test Requirements

"First articles" are preproduction models, test samples, and pilot models that are tested to ensure that the item conforms to contractual requirements before or during the initial stage of production.[315] Testing normally concludes with a first article test ("FAT") report produced either by the Government or the contractor, depending on the contract clause. The FAT must be performed by a specified date, and the contracting officer must approve, reject, or conditionally approve the first article. Regardless of the contracting

---

[314] FAR 4.705.

[315] FAR 9.301.

officer's approval, the contractor is responsible for delivering the first article on time. Failure to deliver on time (or failure to be approved by the contracting officer) means that the contractor "shall be deemed to have failed to make delivery within the meaning of the Default clause of this contract."[316] Under the Default clause, the contract may be terminated immediately upon notification from the Government, without any period to "cure" the defect. It is therefore essential that the contractor pay strict attention to FAT requirements, demonstrate and test an acceptable article, or obtain a new FAT delivery date with the approval of the contracting officer.

C. Unilateral Government Options

An option is a unilateral right in a contract by which, for a specified period of time, the Government may elect to purchase additional supplies or services, or may elect to extend the term of the contract.[317] Options include such things as additional quantities beyond the Government's immediate needs or financial capabilities when the contract was awarded, extension of a service contract for a period of up to six months while a bid protest is being adjudicated or a competition conducted for a new contractor, or the continuation of a contract awarded for a "base year" (the first year) plus up to four option years (e.g., for trash removal, guard services, consulting services).

By exercising an option, and after complying with the FAR requirements,[318] the contracting officer can continue to obtain services or supplies without going through a new procurement. For this reason, the cost of contract options is normally evaluated as part of the price of the initial contract.[319]

The Government has a unilateral right either to exercise options for additional duration or quantity or to ignore them. In order to exercise an option, the Government must comply with the notice requirements in the contract. For example, if the contracting officer decides to extend the term of the contract, he or she must provide the contractor with a preliminary written

---

[316] FAR 52.209-3(d).

[317] FAR 2.101.

[318] FAR 17.207.

[319] FAR 52.217-5.

notice of intent to extend at least 60 days before the contract expires.[320] The provision makes the notice mandatory; without the notice the Government cannot extend the contract.[321] However, as stated in the contract language, preliminary notice does not commit the Government to an extension; that occurs only with the issuance of a formal written order or modification.

A contractor should insist that the Government provide any written notice within the period required and any actual exercise of the option through a written modification or order prior to the date for option exercise.

D. Davis-Bacon Act and Service Contract Act

Construction contracts performed subject to the Davis-Bacon Act[322] or contracts for services performed subject to the Service Contract Act of 1965[323] impose special requirements on the contractor. Failure to comply may result in debarment (i.e., making the contractor ineligible to receive new Government contracts). The fundamental requirement is that the contractor and any subcontractors pay certain minimum wages and benefits according to the wage determination prepared by the Department of Labor ("DOL") and included in the contract (i.e., the prevailing wage rates). For contracts covered by Davis-Bacon, the contractor must submit certified payrolls each

---

[320] FAR 52.217-9.

[321] The notice requirement may be waived by the contractor, and the Government would then be able to exercise the option.

"As option holder, the Government possesses what is generally called a power of acceptance. The option binds the [Government] to do nothing but grants it the right to accept or reject the offer therein in accordance with its terms within the time and in the manner specified in the option. In order to bind the [contractor], 'the notice by which the power of [the Government] is exercised must be unconditional and in exact accord with the terms of the option.' Nothing less will suffice, unless the [contractor] waives one or more of the option's terms. It is settled that the exercise or 'acceptance of an option [by the Government], to be effectual, must be unqualified, absolute, unconditional, unequivocal, unambiguous, positive, without reservation, and [strictly] according to the terms or conditions of the option.'" *Freightliner Corp.*, ASBCA No. 42982, 98-2 BCA ¶ 30,026.

[322] 40 U.S.C. §§ 3141–3148.

[323] 41 U.S.C. § 351 et seq.

week showing wages and benefits paid.[324] On both Davis-Bacon and Service Contract Act contracts, the contractor is subject to reviews and audits by the DOL.

The DOL may examine contractor compliance with wage determinations on its own initiative or based on employee complaints. If the DOL finds noncompliance, it can request that the contracting officer withhold payments in the amount of the estimated wage underpayment or even suspend payment completely pending resolution of the DOL's audit. In addition, upon finding a violation of either of the acts, the Secretary of Labor is required by law to request that the contractor be debarred for three years, absent "unusual circumstances" such as arithmetic error or minor mistake.[325]

The consequences of failure to comply with these labor laws can be severe: rigorous audit by the DOL, withholding of payments due under the contract, and possible three-year debarment. Contractors should cooperate fully with DOL auditors, demonstrate accuracy in payrolls, and explain unusual circumstances that may have caused mistakes.

E. Inspection, Acceptance and Quality Control

A vital element of contract administration is ensuring that the supplies or services delivered to the Government meet fully the contract requirements. An effective inspection and quality assurance/quality control system, established prior to contract performance, is one way to help guarantee such compliance. The Government has a right to reject any goods that do not conform to the contract requirements, except in special circumstances.[326] This is generally known as the "strict compliance" standard.[327] The Government is only required to pay for goods and services that are accepted.

---

[324] FAR 22.406-6(a).

[325] 41 U.S.C. § 351 *et seq.*

[326] FAR 46.407(a).

[327] *Hannon Elec. Co. v. United States*, 31 Fed. Cl. 135, 147 (1994).

The contractor's duties are stated succinctly in the FAR:

- control quality;

- give the Government only supplies and services that conform to contract requirements;

- ensure that its suppliers have an acceptable quality control system; and

- maintain substantiating evidence when the contract requires that supplies or services conform to contract quality requirements, and provide such information to the Government when requested.[328]

Quality control relates to manufacturing processes, drawings, specifications and engineering charges, testing and examination, reliability and maintainability, fabrication, documentation, packaging, procedures, and processes. The contractor is responsible for performing all inspections and tests required by the contract, except those specifically reserved for the Government.

Government contracts require three different levels of quality control systems, depending on the nature of the product or service and on the contractor's system for inspections: (1) commercial quality assurance systems for commercial items; (2) standard inspection requirements for noncommercial items; and (3) higher-level contract quality requirements for complex and critical items.[329] In all three cases the Government relies on the contractor's system for inspections, except in special cases requiring Government inspection. Even in the latter cases, the Government has no duty to inspect. While the Government always retains the right to inspect and check up on the contractor's quality control system, it may elect solely to rely on the contractor's system.

A detailed prescription for quality control and inspection systems is beyond the scope of this book. In general, every contractor must read the contract and design a quality control and inspection system to meet the objectives. Failure of quality control systems and manipulation of testing are

---

[328] FAR 46.105(a).

[329] FAR 46.202.

frequent sources of Government criminal fraud investigations when the contractor provides substandard products to the Government (i.e., engages in product substitution), or delivers inferior or nonconforming goods or services to the Government. The crimes charged are primarily those outlined in Chapter 1.

F. Commercial Items and Services

Agencies are required to conduct market research to determine if commercial items are available to meet agency requirements, and must acquire such items when they are available to meet agency needs.[330] Part 12 of the FAR prescribes policies for the acquisition of commercial items, and this part of the FAR takes precedence over all other FAR sections if there is a conflict.[331] Generally, when contracting for commercial items, the Government is required to use Standard Form 1449, Solicitation/Contract/ Order for Commercial items.[332]

Agencies are required to use firm-fixed-price contracts or fixed-price contracts with economic price adjustment for the acquisition of commercial items; the use of cost-reimbursement type contracts is explicitly prohibited.[333] Of course, indefinite-delivery contracts may be used, but they must be fixed unit price, or fixed unit price with economic price adjustment.[334] Furthermore, contracts for commercial items are required to rely on the contractor's existing quality assurance systems as a substitute for Government inspection and testing, and any in-process inspection by the Government in commercial contracts must be consistent with commercial practices.[335] The Government not only requires the use of SF 1449 in commercial contracts, but requires the use of standard terms and conditions. The Government must use FAR 52.214-5, Contract Terms and Conditions—Commercial Items, a clause which is generally consistent with customary

---

[330] FAR 12.101.

[331] FAR 12.102(c).

[332] FAR 12.204(a).

[333] FAR 12.207.

[334] *Id.*

[335] FAR 12.208.

commercial practices. In addition, the Government must include FAR 52.215-5, Contract Terms and Conditions Required to Implement Statutes or Executive Orders—Commercial Items, which incorporates by reference only the clauses required to implement provisions of law or executive orders applicable to commercial items. The Government is generally permitted to include in a commercial contract only the clauses specified for commercial contracts in FAR Part 12; however, the Government may tailor FAR 52.212-4, but only in a manner that is consistent with "customary commercial practice for the item being acquired" unless the contracting officer obtains a specific waiver.[336] Commercial contracts are also required to use a standard contract format spelled out in FAR 12.303.

The standard commercial provisions include paragraphs titled "Termination for the Government's Convenience"[337] and "Termination for Cause."[338] However, the usual requirements for terminations, which are contained in FAR Part 49, do not apply when terminating commercial item contracts.[339] The Government's rights after a termination for cause includes all remedies available to any buyer in the marketplace, but the preferred method is to acquire similar items from another contractor and to charge the defaulted contractor with any excess reprocurement costs, together with any incidental or consequential damages incurred because of the termination.[340]

Consistent with the provisions of Article 2 of the Uniform Commercial Code ("UCC"), the law governing virtually all commercial sales transactions in the United States, the Government's post-award rights contained in commercial item contracts are the implied warranty of merchantability, the implied warranty of fitness for particular purpose, and the remedies contained in the acceptance paragraph.[341] There is one significant difference, namely, that the UCC permits sellers to vary the terms of these warranties,[342] while in a Government commercial item contract, *they may not be*

---

[336] FAR 12.302(c).

[337] FAR 52.212-4(l).

[338] FAR 52.212-4(m).

[339] FAR 12.403(a).

[340] FAR 12.403(c)(2).

[341] FAR 12.404(a).

[342] U.C.C. § 2-316.

varied, except where it is customary commercial practice for contractors to exclude or limit the implied warranties in the provisions of an express warranty. In such cases, the contracting officer is required to ensure that the express warranty provides for the repair or replacement of defective items discovered within a reasonable period of time after acceptance.[343]

The *implied warranty of merchantability* provides that an item is reasonably fit for the ordinary purposes for which such items are used. The items must be of at least average, fair or medium-grade quality and must be comparable in quality to those that will pass without objection in the trade or market for items of the same description.[344]

The *implied warranty of fitness for a particular purpose* provides that an item is fit for use for the particular purpose for which the Government will use the items. The Government can rely upon an implied warranty of fitness for particular purpose when: (1) the seller knows the particular purpose for which the Government intends to use the item; and (2) the Government relied upon the contractor's skill and judgment that the item would be appropriate for that particular purpose.[345]

The Federal Acquisition Streamlining Act of 1994[346] requires contracting officers to take advantage of commercial warranties, and to obtain, to the maximum extent practicable, at least the same warranty terms, including offers of extended warranties, offered to the general public in customary commercial practice.[347] Any such express warranties must be included in the contract by addendum.[348]

Finally, the Government is extremely limited in the types of subcontract clauses that it may require on a commercial item contract. The commercial item contract must include FAR 52.244-6, "Subcontracts for Commercial Items and Commercial Components," and this clause specifically states that

---

[343] FAR 12.404(b)(2).

[344] FAR 12.404(a)(1).

[345] FAR 12.404(a)(2).

[346] Pub. L. No. 103-355; 41 U.S.C. § 264 note.

[347] FAR 12.404(b).

[348] FAR 12.404(b)(3).

"[n]otwithstanding any other clause of this contract, the Contractor is not required to include any FAR provision or clause" except for FAR 52.219-8, Utilization of Small Business Concerns; 52.222-26, Equal Opportunity (E.O. 11246); 52.222-35, Affirmative Action for Disabled Veterans and Veterans of the Vietnam Era (38 U.S.C. § 4212(a)); 52.222-36, Affirmative Action for Workers with Disabilities (29 U.S.C. § 793); and 52.247-64, Preference for Privately Owned U.S.-Flag Commercial Vessels."[349] Furthermore, the contractor must include FAR 52.244-6 in all subcontracts, thereby limiting the flowdown of clauses that may be made to second-tier subcontractors.[350]

G. Government Property

The Government frequently owns property that it makes available to Government contractors for the performance of their contract. FAR Part 45 prescribes various policies and procedures for such items, which includes both real and personal property, facilities, material, special tooling, special test equipment, and agency-peculiar equipment.[351]

Contractors are responsible and liable for Government property in their possession, unless their contract specifies otherwise.[352] The Government retains title to all Government-furnished property.[353] The contractor is responsible and accountable for all Government property it receives (including property that is provided to the prime contractor's subcontractors), and must establish and maintain a program for the use, maintenance, repair, protection and preservation of Government property in accordance with sound industrial practice.[354] The contractor's program must be in writing, and must be approved by the Government property administrator.[355]

---

[349] FAR 52.244-6(c).

[350] FAR 52.244-6(d).

[351] FAR 45.101.

[352] FAR 45.103(a).

[353] FAR 52.245-2(c).

[354] FAR 45.502(a) and FAR 52.245-2(e).

[355] Id.

Contractors must maintain adequate control records for all Government property.[356]

The contractor is responsible for the proper care, maintenance and use of Government property from the time of receipt until return.[357] Government property may only be used for the purposes authorized in the contract.[358] Subject to the terms of the contract and the particular circumstances, the contractor may be liable for shortages, loss, damages or destruction of Government property, or when use or consumption unreasonably exceeds allowances provided in the contract.[359]

H. Cost Principles—Primarily for Cost-Reimbursement Contracts and Cost Principles for Change Orders

1. Cost Accounting Standards

Certain Government contracts are subject to the Cost Accounting Standards ("CAS"), a set of financial rules that requires, among other things, that contractors disclose in writing and follow consistently their cost accounting practices.[360] There are 19 different standards, covering such matters as consistency in allocating costs, accounting for unallowed costs, depreciation, pension costs, cost of money, direct and indirect costs, and insurance costs.

Detailed discussion of CAS is beyond the scope of this book, but the contractor must determine at the outset if the contract is subject to CAS and, if so, take steps to comply with CAS. Among these steps is to obtain the appropriate professional services to ensure CAS compliance. The following are the major types of contracts that are *exempt* from all CAS requirements:

---

[356] FAR 45.505(a).

[357] FAR 45.509.

[358] FAR 45.509-2(a)(1).

[359] FAR 45.504(a).

[360] 48 C.F.R. Chapter 99; FAR Part 30.

- Sealed-bid contracts;

- Contracts and subcontracts with small business;

- Negotiated contracts and subcontracts of $500,000 or less;

- Firm-fixed-price contracts and subcontracts awarded without submission of any cost data; and

- Contracts and subcontracts for commercial items.[361]

2. Reasonable, Allocable, and Allowable Incurred Costs

For cost-reimbursement contracts, the FAR indicates that costs are allowed (i.e., may be charged to the contract) to the extent they are reasonable, allocable, and allowable[362] under certain FAR sections.[363] This is particularly important to defense contractors that may be subject to penalties for submitting unallowable indirect costs in final indirect cost rate proposals or the final statement of costs incurred in a fixed-price incentive contract.[364] All contractors, however, should ensure that they charge the Government only appropriate and allowable costs.

A cost (either direct or indirect) is *reasonable* if "in its nature and amount, it does not exceed that which would be incurred by a prudent person in the conduct of competitive business."[365] A cost is *allocable* if it is assignable to one or more cost objectives on the basis of relative benefits received.[366] Specifically, it is allocable if: (1) it is incurred expressly for the contract, (2) benefits both the contract and other work and can be distributed in proportion to benefits received, or (3) is necessary to the overall operation of the business. A FAR section on selected costs lists 52 different categories

---

[361] 48 C.F.R. § 9903.201-1(b).

[362] FAR 31.204(a).

[363] FAR 31.201, 31.202, 31.203, and 31.205.

[364] 10 U.S.C. § 2324(a)–(d); FAR 42.709.

[365] FAR 31.201-3.

[366] FAR 31.201-4.

of cost—such as public relations, bad debts, personal services, depreciation, contingencies, entertainment, consultant, relocation, taxes—and describes in detail which costs are allowable and unallowable.[367]

Contractors should study the regulations and establish a cost accounting system in advance of contract award. After award, all invoices and requests for progress payments should be prepared in keeping with requirements for allowable costs.

I. Payment

1. Types of Payment

There are two major types of payment: (1) payment of the contact price for completed and accepted items of work and (2) progress payments based upon costs incurred or a percentage of completion of the work.

a. Payment of the Price

Payment of the contract price is due upon the completion and acceptance of the work and submission of a proper invoice or voucher. This is similar to private contracts. A contract may authorize "partial payments" for delivery and acceptance of complete units or distinct items of service. This method of payment is not considered a financing technique but does serve as an important means of providing funds for performance. Only with straight fixed-price contracts is the price firm at the outset. More often, many fixed-priced contracts are subject to redetermination of the price during or after performance. Fixed-price contracts of this type include fixed-price incentive contracts or price redetermination contracts. See Chapter 2 for a discussion of types of contracts. In these types of contracts, the target prices are used as billing prices. Such payments are provisional in nature and adjusted if circumstances change.

---

[367] FAR 31.205.

b. Progress Payments

Progress payments are of two types—those based on costs and those based on completion of work. Progress payments based on costs have traditionally been included in contracts over $1 million ($100,000 for small businesses) which require a substantial amount of time between the beginning of performance and completion. The contractor is entitled to recover a stipulated percentage of its own costs plus the amount of progress payments made to subcontractors. Currently, the "customary progress payment rate" is 80 percent for large businesses and 85 percent for small businesses.[368] Progress payments are recouped by the Government through "liquidation" or the deduction of such progress amounts from payments that would otherwise be due to contractors for completed contract items.

Progress payments based on percentage of completion are used for contracts for construction, shipbuilding, and ship conversion, alteration, or repair.[369] Under this method, the Government makes progress payments monthly as the work proceeds or at more frequent intervals as determined by the contracting officer.[370]

2. Financing Techniques

Part 32 of the FAR provides for a variety of financing techniques that may be used in Government contracts. When the Government purchases commercial items,[371] financing is usually the responsibility of the contractor.[372] However, when the contracting officer determines it is appropriate or

---

[368] FAR 32.501-1.

[369] DFARS 232.102.

[370] See FAR 52.232-5.

[371] Commercial items are items of a type customarily used for non-governmental purposes and that have been offered or sold, leased, or licensed to the public; items that evolved from such items or that include minor modifications made to meet federal requirements; and services offered competitively in substantial quantities in the commercial market place under standard commercial terms. See FAR 2.101 for the complete definition of "commercial item."

[372] FAR 32.202-1.

customary in the commercial marketplace, the contractor may receive commercial advance payments[373] and commercial progress payments.[374]

The principal types of noncommercial-item purchase financing include advance payments, progress payments, and assignment of claims. As mentioned above, partial payments also serve as a way to finance perform-ance but are not technically a financing method. *Advance payments* are advances of money by the Government to a prime contractor before, in anticipation of, and for the purpose of performance under a contract.[375] The Government will provide for advance payments (considered the "least preferred method of contract financing")[376] for noncommercial items where there is adequate security given and in very special circumstances, such as contracts for the management of Government-owned plants or highly classified contracts.[377]

Normally, for simplified acquisitions (under $100,000), the Government provides no contract financing.[378] In some markets, however, the provision of financing is a commercial practice. In these circumstances, the FAR permits the use of commercial progress payments and commercial advance payments where they are in the best interests of the Government.[379]

Assignment of claims is a financing technique whereby a contractor may borrow from a financing institution in order to perform a particular contract and assign all of the proceeds of that contract to the financing institution. The financing institution will then deduct payments owed and remit the balance to the contractor. Government contractors are prohibited from

---

[373] Commercial advance payments are payments made before any work is performed under the contract and are limited to 15 percent of the contract price. FAR 32.202-2.

[374] Commercial progress payments are normally given to the contractor after some work has been done.

[375] FAR 32.102.

[376] FAR 32.402.

[377] FAR 32.403.

[378] FAR 32.003.

[379] FAR 32.202-1.

assigning the actual performance of a contract to another contractor.[380] However, they may avail themselves of this financing technique in order to obtain a loan. The FAR provides specific procedures and formats that must be used in order to perfect the assignment.[381]

Contractors should take full advantage of financing opportunities. If progress payments are authorized, requests for them should be submitted as frequently as allowed (normally monthly). If not, the assignment of claims procedure can furnish operating capital. This is a very common method of financing Government contracts. A contractor selling commercial items that is fortunate enough to obtain advance or progress payments (and fortunate enough to have a willing contracting officer) could exploit either or both methods and maximize its cash flow throughout contract performance.

3. Payment Procedures

a. Invoices and Vouchers

The first step in the payment process is the submission of a request for payment. This is generally done by the submission of an invoice or voucher. These terms are sometimes used synonymously; although "invoice" means a bill or written request for payment for work or services performed under the contract while "voucher" denotes a recording of a business transaction, such as an expense voucher. Vouchers are routinely submitted for payments under cost-reimbursement contracts.

In order to get paid, a contractor must submit a *proper* invoice. A proper invoice consists of the following information:

1. Name of contractor and invoice date (contractors are encouraged to date invoices as close as possible to the date of mailing or transmission);

2. Contract number, or other authorization for delivery of property or services (assignment of an invoice number by the contractor is recommended);

---

[380] 41 U.S.C. § 15(a).

[381] *See* FAR 32.805.

3. Description, price, and quantity of property and services actually delivered or rendered;

4. Shipping and payment terms;

5. Other substantiating documentation or information as required by the contract (e.g., a proper certificate showing acceptance, such as a DD Form 250, Material Inspection and Receiving Report); and

6. Name (where practicable), title, telephone number, and complete mailing address of responsible official to whom payment is to be sent.[382]

b. Receiving Reports

"Receiving reports" are used to document the completion of work or receipt of supplies. This report, along with the contractor's invoice, constitute the necessary documentation in order to get paid. Receiving reports must be forwarded to the designated payment office within five days. The receiving report must contain the following information:

1. Contract or other authorization number;

2. Product or service description;

3. Quantities received, if applicable;

4. Date(s) property or services delivered and accepted; and

5. Signature (or electronic alternative when supported by appropriate internal controls), printed name, title, telephone number, and mailing address of the receiving official.[383]

---

[382] OMB Circular A-125, § 5(c) (superceded and rescinded by 5 C.F.R. § 1315.9(b)).

[383] 5 C.F.R. § 1315.9(c).

c. Payment Authority

The receiving report and invoice are forwarded to the "disbursing official" for payment. Note that while contracting officers have authority to enter into contracts which obligate the United States, they do not have the authority to disburse monies.[384] Generally only employees designated as "disbursing officials" may disburse public monies.[385] The disbursing official will examine the voucher to determine if its in proper form, that its certified and approved, and that its computed correctly. Prior to the disbursing official taking action a certifying officer must verify the invoice. This entails confirming the information on the invoice, such as name of the payee and the allowability of the expense. Both the certifying and disbursing officials may be held liable for improper payment.

4. Prompt Payment

The Government must make payment either (1) on the date(s) specified in the contract or (2) if a payment date is not specified in the contract, 30 days after the Government receives a proper invoice for the amount due.[386] If the Government is "late" in making payment, then it must pay interest as required by the Prompt Payment Act.[387] In order to calculate the payment due date it is necessary to determine when the invoice or voucher was received. The agency is considered to have received an invoice on the later of (1) the date the person designated by the agency to first receive such invoice actually receives a proper invoice or (2) on the seventh day after the date on which the property is actually delivered or performance is actually completed.[388] Payment is deemed to occur "on the date a check for payment

---

[384] 31 U.S.C. § 3321.

[385] *Id.*

[386] 31 U.S.C. § 3903(a)(1); 5 C.F.R. § 1315.

[387] This interest rate is established by the Secretary of the Treasury pursuant to 31 U.S.C. § 3902(a). The rate may be found at http://www.publicdebt.treas.gov/opd/opdprm2.htm.

[388] 31 U.S.C. § 3901(a)(4).

is dated or an electronic fund transfer is made"—*not upon the contractor's receipt of a Government check.*[389]

J. Subcontracts and Flowdowns

Many Government contracts are quite complex and require prime contractors to obtain assistance from other contractors in order to fully perform. A common method is the use of subcontracts between the prime contractor and a subcontractor. A subcontractor is generally any firm that supplies materials or performs services for a prime contractor, pursuant to the requirements of a Government contract. This section explains the important principles of prime contractor-subcontractor relationships.

1. Contractual Relationships and the Rights and Responsibilities of Subcontractors—Privity

In order to enforce contractual rights between parties to any contract, there must first be a direct contractual relationship between the two parties. This direct relationship is known as "privity of contract." It is a fundamental principle of Government contracting that the Government is in privity with (i.e., has a direct contractual relationship) *only* the prime contractor, except in special situations that need not be discussed in this book. For a depiction of the privity relationship see **Figure 4-4**.

From this basic premise flows two equally fundamental principles: (1) because it is not in privity with a subcontractor, the Government cannot enforce its rights directly by demanding certain performance or actions be taken by a subcontractor; rather, the Government must make the demands of the prime contractor, and the prime contractor must then require the subcontractor to perform; and (2) because the subcontractor is not in privity with the Government, it cannot seek remedies directly from the Government; rather, it must seek its remedies through the prime contractor, who may or may not seek redress from the Government.

The subcontract between the prime and subcontractor is essentially a special kind of commercial contract between two commercial entities, and is governed by the appropriate state laws. To be sure, the subcontract will

---

[389] 31 U.S.C. § 3901(a)(5).

probably include Government standards, Government prime contract clauses, and other matters taken from the prime's contract with the Government; however, the subcontract is merely a commercial contract since *neither* party to it is a "Government."

The prime contractor continuously acts as a buffer between the Government and the subcontractor. The Government cannot direct the subcontractor to do something, nor may the Government issue a change order to a subcontractor and demand that it be followed. The Government must issue directions and change orders to the prime contractor, which in turn, must direct (or issue changes) to its subcontractor. The subcontractor must keep this in mind during its performance, and must be careful *not* to take direction from the Government, but must take its direction and changes only from the prime contractor. A subcontractor that changes its specifications, delivery date, or quantity based on Government direction cannot expect to be compensated by the prime contractor from such changes. The prime contractor may rightfully point to the terms of the subcontract and demand that they be enforced, unless they are changed by the prime contractor.

The lack of privity between a subcontractor and the Government also gives rise to another principle, which is that the subcontractor must seek remedies for additional costs, changes in scope, schedule or specifications, *from the prime contractor, not from the Government.*[390] Just as the Government may not direct changes from a subcontractor, the subcontractor cannot collect from the Government directly for changes imposed by the prime contractor. In fact, most changes imposed by the prime on the subcontractor result from Government direction to the prime contractor, therefore, the prime contractor will have recourse against Government, but the subcontractor will not. The subcontractor must seek remedies from the prime contractor, with whom he is in privity, normally in state or federal courts that have jurisdiction over such matters.

---

[390] A subcontractor may, however, seek a claim through sponsorship by the prime contractor. *Erickson Air Crane Co. of Washington, Inc. v. United States,* 731 F.2d 810 (Fed. Cir. 1984).

Privity of Contract-Rights and
Responsibilities of Subcontractors

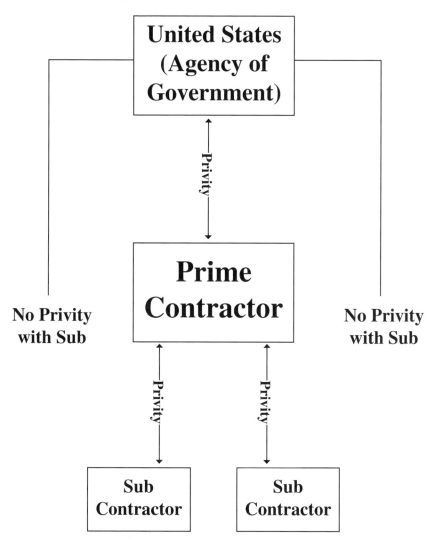

Figure 4.4

2. *Government Controls Over Subcontracting and Subcontractors*

Although the Government is generally not in privity with the subcontractor, it may use other methods to exercise some form of control over them. One way, described above, is for the Government to order the prime contractor to do or change something which the Government knows is being performed by a subcontractor. The prime contractor would then be obligated to order the subcontractor to take the action or to make the change that the Government requires.

The Government exercises control in other ways as well, including: (1) the Government may insist on a right to review the prime contractor's purchasing systems to ensure that the subcontracts are efficiently awarded; (2) the Government may require that the prime contractor obtain the Government's consent prior to the award of subcontracts; and (3) the Government may, through the operation of law or the actual terms of the prime contract themselves, require that the prime contractor "flow down" to the subcontractor a significant number of clauses that are in the prime contract. Each of these methods of controlling the prime and subcontractor are discussed below.

a. *Government Purchasing Systems Reviews*

The purpose of a contractor purchasing system review ("CPSR") by the Government is to "evaluate the efficiency and effectiveness with which the contractor spends Government funds and complies with Government policy when subcontracting."[391] Based on the CPSR, the contracting officer can grant, withhold, or withdraw approval of the contractor's purchasing system.

During a CPSR, the Government evaluates the contractor's purchasing system to determine the degree of price competition obtained, pricing policies and techniques (how accurate, complete and current the sub's cost and pricing data are); how well the responsibility of the subcontractors is determined by the prime; appropriateness of types of contracts used; management control systems, planning award and postaward management; compliance with cost accounting standards, and policies and procedures

---

[391] FAR 44.301.

pertaining to small business concerns.[392] When a contractor's purchasing system is not approved, the contractor can expect more frequent audits and far more frequent surveillance by Government employees.

b. Government Consent to Subcontracts

If the contractor does not have an approved purchasing system, Government consent to subcontract is required for any cost-reimbursement, time and materials, labor hour or letter contract, and also for unpriced actions (including modifications) that exceed the simplified acquisition threshold.[393] If the contractor has an approved purchasing system, consent to subcontract is required only for subcontracts specifically identified by the contracting officer in the subcontracts clause of the contract.[394] Under cost-reimbursement contracts, even if the contractor has an approved purchasing system and consent to subcontracting is not required for reasons stated above, the contractor is required by statute[395] to notify the agency before award of any cost-plus-fixed-fee subcontract or any fixed-price subcontract that exceeds $100,000 or 5 percent of the total estimated cost of the contract.[396]

c. Flowdowns of Government Contract Clauses to the Subcontract

Certain clauses in the Government's prime contract must be flowed down, i.e., incorporated into the subcontracts awarded by the prime. These clauses are designed to protect the Government's rights and interest and to promote Government policies.

---

[392] FAR 44.303.

[393] FAR 44.201-1(b). The simplified acquisition threshold is presently $100,000.

[394] FAR 44.201-1(a).

[395] 10 U.S.C. § 2306(e) or 41 U.S.C. § 254(b).

[396] FAR 44.201-2.

Some clauses explicitly mandate flowdown to the subcontracts (e.g., the Audit Clause, FAR 52.215-2;[397] the Cost Accounting Standards Clause, FAR 52.230-2; the Equal Opportunity clauses, FAR 52.222-6), while other clauses implicitly require the flowdown (e.g., the Davis-Bacon Act, FAR 52.222-6;[398] and the Service Contract Act of 1965 clause, FAR 52.222-41[399]).

Strangely enough, the Government does not require, either implicitly or explicitly, the flowdown of the Changes clause (FAR 52.243-1) or the Termination for Convenience of the Government clause (FAR 52.249-2). Not including these clauses in the subcontractor contract may have serious future ramifications. If these two causes are not flowed down, the prime contractor will be unable to terminate the subcontractor in the event of a Government convenience termination, and the prime contractor will be unable (absent what could be a monumental price increase) to change the specifications, delivery date or quantity, in response to a Government-ordered change order.[400] Remember, the subcontract is a commercial contract between two commercial entities, and is subject to the Uniform Commercial Code and state laws. The concepts of "change" or "termination for convenience" are not part of commercial contracts, which require mutual agreement by the parties in order to change any term of an existing contract.[401]

Prime contractors are advised to examine their contracts carefully, and whenever there is a doubt in their mind, flow down the prime contract clause to the subcontractor, making appropriate changes in the text. This is

---

[397] "The Contractor shall insert a clause containing all the terms of this clause . . . in all subcontracts under this contract [under most conditions]." FAR 52.215-2(g)(1).

[398] "All laborers and mechanics employed or working upon the site of the [including all subcontractors] will be paid [a minimum wage]."

[399] "Each service employee employed in the performance of this contract by the Contractor or any subcontractor shall be paid "certain minimum wages."

[400] The Termination for Default clause at FAR 52.249-8 should also be flowed down, although it is not as important to do so in light of the Uniform Commercial Code Part 6 (Breach) and Part 7 (Remedies), which apply to the subcontracts.

[401] U.C.C. § 2-209.

normally accomplished by incorporating the text of the clause by reference in the subcontract by its FAR clause number and title and by stating in the subcontract that "the clauses are incorporated herein by reference with the same force and effect as if set forth in full text." Furthermore, the subcontract should also include a statement that explains that whenever the term "Government or Contracting Officer" appears in the clause, it shall be replaced by "Prime Contractor;" and whenever the term "contractor or prime contractor" appears in the clause, it shall be replaced by "subcontractor."

d. Subcontracts for Commercial Items

Contracts for commercial items are required to include the clause at FAR 52.244-6, Subcontracts for Commercial items and Commercial Components. This clause indicates that subcontractors need only include five clauses in any subcontracts that it awards.[402] This considerably simplifies subcontracts for commercial items.

e. Construction Contract Payments to Subcontractors

One final way that the Government controls prime contractor's actions with subcontractors is the inclusion of a certification in FAR 52.232-5, Payments Under Fixed-Price Construction Contracts. This certification states that "Payments to subcontractors and supplies have been made from previous payments received under the contract, and timely payments will be made from the proceeds of the payments covered by this certification."[403]

3. The Importance of Subcontracts

Subcontracts are likely to be essential to the performance of your Government contract. It is essential that a prime contractor purchase from

---

[402] These clauses are FAR 52.219-8, Utilization of Small Business Concerns; FAR 52.226-26, Equal Opportunity (E.O. 11246), FAR 52.222-35, Affirmative Action for Disabled Veterans and Veterans of the Vietnam Era; FAR 53.222-36, Affirmative Action for Workers with Disabilities; and FAR 52.247-64, Preference for Privately Owned U.S.-Flag Vessels.

[403] FAR 52.232-5(c)(2).

suppliers and subcontractors pursuant to a written contract or purchase order. Furthermore, it is essential that the subcontractor or purchase order flow down all required contract clauses required to be flowed down by law, regulation or prime contract. In addition, as previously stated, the subcontract or purchase order *must flow down the changes clause, the termination for convenience clause and termination for default clause.* Failure to include these crucial clauses may result in serious financial and commercial consequences to the prime contractor.

Contractors may draft their own subcontracts, or they may use the excellent text provided in the American Bar Association ("ABA") Model Fixed-Price Supply Subcontract Form, which may be obtained from the ABA.

K. Contract Closeout

The final step in the contract administration process is "contract closeout." Once work is completed and accepted and after the contractor has submitted a proper invoice, which is then certified by the certifying officer and sent to the disbursing officer, final payment is made. Final payment is significant because it generally discharges all of the rights and obligations of the parties under the contract. Sometimes, however, there is a delay is making final payment due to a delay in finalizing negotiated overhead rates.

L. Audits and Investigations

1. Audits

Audits are serious matters for many reasons. An audit can slow or stop contract payments, for example, and auditors frequently refer potential fraud cases to investigators, including Inspectors General ("IGs"). There are many different "auditors," including those in the Wage and Hour Division of the Department of Labor ("DOL") who audit labor records, contract auditors from the Defense Contract Audit Agency, IG auditors from the various IG offices, and cost and price analysts who perform analyses similar to audits on behalf of the contracting officer.

Contractors should cooperate with auditors but should not disclose more information than required by the law, the FAR, and the contract's specific audit clauses.[404] In addition to examining contractor records, auditors frequently seek to perform "floor checks" or interviews of selected employees to ascertain how company records are maintained. In dealing with auditors, a contractor should take the following precautions:

1. Insist on an "entrance briefing" on the audit scope and objectives before the audit begins and an "exit briefing" at the conclusion of the audit to provide the contractor with the audit findings. If any auditor appears to be exceeding the stated scope, discuss it with the auditor. If not satisfied or if the briefings are not offered, contact the auditor's supervisor.

2. Deliver records to auditors in a room designated solely for that purpose. Do not permit auditors to wander around the contractor's place of business.

3. Advise employees of audits, and indicate to them that auditors are to be given full cooperation. However, emphasize that all auditor requests for documents must go through the company's "audit focal point," who must keep track of all documents given to auditors.

4. Do not give auditors access to company copying facilities. Ask them to mark the items they want copied and have the audit focal point copy them.

2. Investigations

A criminal investigation is perhaps the gravest situation a contractor can face. Most contract investigations conducted by an IG or the FBI are fraud investigations, designed to determine if the contractor has made false statements in obtaining or performing the contract, has made false claims to the Government, has made false representations in the bid, or has in some other way defrauded the Government. (See Chapter 1 for a list of statutes most frequently used in prosecuting Government contractors.) An investigation is probably underway if: (1) there is heightened audit activity; (2) investigators (special agents) from the FBI or IG's office visit employees (usually at their homes, not in the office); or (3) the contractor receives a

---

[404] FAR 52.214-26, FAR 52.215-2, and FAR 52.212-5.

subpoena—either an IG subpoena for documents or a grand jury subpoena for documents and/or testimony.

Upon learning of an investigation, the contractor should tell employees to prepare for the possibility of being interviewed by a special agent, warn them to tell the truth, inform them of their right to have an attorney present during any interview, and remind them that they have the right to decline to speak with investigators at all. If company policy is to pay for counsel in such situations, employees should be so advised. Also, the company should remind employees that company documents may not be shown or given to any investigation without written consent from company counsel or the president of the company. Ideally, much valuable information has already been communicated to contractor employees through a soundly written company ethics code and comprehensive employee training.

M. Summary: Rules for Day-to-Day Contract Administration

1.   Develop and use a proper records management program.

2.   Establish an effective inspection/quality control system that complies with all requirements of the contract.

3.   Determine if the Cost Accounting Standards apply and, if so, follow them precisely.

4.   In cost-reimbursement contracts, charge to the contract only reasonable, allocable, and allowable costs.

5.   Honor FAT requirements, including FAT delivery date.

6.   Know that options in a contract are unilateral; only the Government can exercise them.

7.   Be especially attentive to labor requirements where the Davis-Bacon Act or Service Contract Act applies.

8.   Make sure any relationship with a subcontractor is in writing either as a written contract or purchase order.

9. Flow down to the subcontract all contract clauses required by law, regulation, or prime contract.

10. Ensure that every contract with a subcontractor contains the Changes clause and the Termination for Convenience of the Government clause.

11. Ensure invoices are properly submitted and contain all necessary information for payment.

12. Make sure receiving reports are forwarded to the designated payment office within five days.

13. Understand that if the Government is late in making payment, then it must pay interest as required by the Prompt Payment Act, and enforce this requirement.

14. Ensure that any Government property entrusted to you under the contract is maintained and preserved in accordance with industrial standards and that adequate controls and records are maintained.

15. Use all available and appropriate payment and financing techniques including, where applicable, advance payments, partial payments, progress payments, and bank financing through assignment of claims.

16. Recognize that audits and investigations have potentially serious consequences and respond promptly and in full compliance with the law when either one is begun.

17. Always cooperate with auditors but do not disclose more information than required by the law, the FAR, and the contract's specific audit clauses.

18. If under investigation, explain to employees that they should prepare for the possibility of being interviewed by a special agent, warn them to tell the truth, and inform them that they have a right to decline to speak to investigators at all, or may have counsel present during any interview they grant.

III. SPECIAL ADMINISTRATIVE MATTERS

A. Changes

1. Government-Ordered Changes

One of the unique aspects of Government contracting is that the Government, through the Changes clause, has the *unilateral* right to "make changes within the general scope of the contract" in the specifications (when the goods are to be specially manufactured for the Government), the method of shipment, or the place of delivery.[405] The purpose of the Changes clause is to give the Government flexibility so that it can adapt to changes in technology or in its needs and requirements (such as closing of military bases and the downsizing of personnel). In commercial contracting, changes of this nature require the agreement of both parties,[406] making it impossible for one party alone to decide that it wants a modification. However, as long as the changes are "within the general scope" of the contract, the Government can order the contractor to make them. The contractor in turn has a right to request an equitable adjustment if the cost of the contract, as modified, exceeds the previously estimated cost of the contract.

Out-of-scope changes are known as "cardinal changes" and involve significant alterations in the nature or amount of work that the contractor bargained for when the contract was formed and is required by the contract to perform. Examples of cardinal changes include: (1) ordering a contractor that was building a fabric filter particle collection system (commonly called a "baghouse"), which extracted pollutants from an airstream, to withstand an internal operating pressure of 1.6 pounds per square inch and a safety range two to four times that pressure; the original contract contained no such requirement;[407] (2) requiring a contractor to rebuild a hangar after the hangar

---

[405] *See, e.g.*, FAR 52.243-1, the Changes clause in fixed-price contracts.

[406] *See, e.g.*, U.C.C. §§ 2-209 and 2-301.

[407] *Airprep Technology, Inc. v. United States*, 30 Fed. Cl. 488, 505 (1994). The court reviewing this change noted that the Government's proposed change would have required closing off the inlet and sealing the blowout doors, meaning that the "baghouse would cease being a baghouse . . . intended to filter a moving stream of air. Treating it like a metal balloon plainly cannot simulate 'operating' conditions."

initially constructed by the contractor had collapsed because of a defective specification; the change involved major reconstruction and almost doubled the contract price;[408] (3) in a contract for construction of a levee, increasing the embankment from 7,950 cubic yards to 13,265 cubic yards of earth, a change that necessitated bringing equipment 100 miles back to the jobsite;[409] and (4) eliminating entirely a building from a hospital complex, causing a 10 percent reduction in contract price.[410]

Whenever the change ordered is deemed a cardinal change, the courts will find that it can be made only through the bilateral consent of both the Government and the contractor; otherwise, it will be considered a breach of the contract.

Only the contracting officer can issue changes to the contract, unless that authority has been delegated, in writing, to an ACO.[411] If the contracting officer issues a change order that the contractor believes is an unfavorable, cardinal change, the contractor should dispute it in writing and attempt to have it withdrawn.

A sample letter appears in **Figure 4-5**. The contractor may further appeal the contracting officer's decision in accordance with the Disputes clause.

---

[408] *Edward R. Marden Corp. v. United States*, 442 F.2d 364, 194 Ct. Cl. 799 (1971).

[409] *P.L. Saddler v. United States*, 287 F.2d 411, 152 Ct. Cl. 557 (1961).

[410] *General Contracting & Constr. Co., Inc. v. United States*, 84 Ct. Cl. 570 (1937).

[411] FAR 43.202.

**LETTER TO CONTRACTING OFFICER ASSERTING
OUT-OF-SCOPE (CARDINAL) CHANGE**

ABC Company
Address

Date

Ms. Jane Doe
Contracting Officer
Address

RE: Contract No. XYZ-123

Dear Ms. Doe:

You have requested that, pursuant to the referenced contract, this company provide base maintenance services at Fort Jones, LA, in addition to similar services at Fort Smythe, MS. Please be advised that neither party contemplated services at any location other than Fort Jones when this contract was competed. Furthermore, Fort Jones is 100 miles away from Fort Smythe and approximately three times as large. Accordingly, your proposed modification exceeds the scope of the contract and may not be issued under the Changes clause.

We request that you withdraw your request to expand services. If you elect not to withdraw, we shall proceed in accordance with the Disputes clause.

Very truly yours,

John Smith
Contractor

Figure 4-5

In some cases, however, a contractor may wish to accept a cardinal change because, for example, the changed work relates to the contract, is expected to be profitable, and can be performed without disruption of the contractor's plans, workforce, and financing. Obviously, in such a case, the contractor would refrain from raising the cardinal-change issue and proceed with the work based on a written change order to the contract. The contractor should make every effort to comply with in-scope change orders, but if it is not possible, the matter should be discussed with the contracting officer and the results documented for the record. Where any change causes an increase or decrease in the cost or the time required for performance of the contract, the contractor should assert the right to an equitable adjustment in writing within 30 days of the receipt of the change order.[412]

A sample letter notifying the contracting officer of a request for equitable adjustment appears in **Figure 4-6**.

LETTER TO CONTRACTING OFFICER ASSERTING
CLAIM FOR EQUITABLE ADJUSTMENT

ABC Company
Address

January 15, 1994

Ms. Jane Doe
Contracting Officer
Address

RE: Contract No. XYZ-123

Dear Ms. Doe:

Modification No. 29 to the referenced contract was received on January 2, 1994, and we are presently implementing the requirement to add weekend guard coverage at Gate 12 of the Post and to provide certain additional services. We shall assert a claim for an equitable adjustment for Modification No. 29. Because of the complexity of the change, we are unable to submit a proposal for an equitable adjustment at this time.

We anticipate submission of this equitable-adjustment request on or about February 28, 1994.

Very truly yours,

John Smith
Contractor

Figure 4-6

---

[412] FAR 52.243-1(c). Note, however, that the contracting officer may "receive and act upon a proposal submitted before final payment" if he or she decides that the facts justify it. *Id.*

2. Written, Signed Changes

As noted previously, normally only the contracting officer has the authority to order changes or modifications in the contract. Should anyone else, such as a quality control official, quality assurance representative, inspector, or contract specialist, order changes, the contractor should immediately verify in writing that this action carries the authority of the contracting officer and that the contractor has the right to assert a request for an equitable adjustment.

A "constructive" change occurs where, through written or oral conduct, the Government requires the contractor to make a change but does not specifically order it pursuant to the Changes clause. The following are examples of constructive changes:

- **Directive to perform additional work**: (1) Government ordered additional wells to be built beyond those included in a contract for design and construction of a river control structure—either through conduct that amounted to an order by threatening the contractor with default or by requiring changes when the Government alleged that the system proved inadequate.[413] (2) Government orally imposed a new standard (15 percent maximum moisture content) on the type of wood that could be used in making an acoustical fence.[414] (3) Government required a consulting services contractor to write extra reports not specified under the contract and to collect extra data.[415]

- **Defective specifications**: Government specified a particular size and weight for electric generators, requiring that the units be capable of operating 23 hours a day for six months with only normal maintenance; Government determined that a generator of the specified design could not meet the performance requirements and changed the design by relaxing the size and weight limitations; con-

---

[413] *Al Johnson Constr. Co. v. United States*, 20 Cl. Ct. 184 (1990).

[414] *Freeman-Darling, Inc.*, GSBCA No. 7112, 89-2 BCA ¶ 21,882.

[415] *Environment Consultants, Inc.*, IBCA No. 1192-5-78, 79-2 BCA ¶ 13,937.

tractor was allowed the costs it incurred in trying to perform in accordance with the original, defective specifications.[416]

- **Incorrect contract interpretation**: Army's contract interpretation
  caused the contractor to repair more windows than contemplated
  under a contract for inspection and repair of window panes in Government warehouses—contract required reputtying where cracking
  was "excessive"; Army required reputtying of all cracks.[417]

- **Limitation on method of performance**: (1) Government refused to
  allow contractor to use steeper excavation slopes as planned under a
  contract for construction of underground parking garages.[418]
  (2) Although contract neither specified nor prohibited the use of any
  particular tool or method for paint removal, Government insisted on
  use of electric heating guns and refused to allow painting contractor
  to use propane torches and chemicals to remove old paint.[419]

- **Unreasonable inspection**: (1) Government inspection exceeded
  scope set forth in contract by demanding uniform appearance and
  100 percent mopping of floors even though contract only called for
  spot mopping of 10 percent of floor area.[420] (2) Government increased the frequency of safety inspections from once a month, as
  set forth in contract, to once a week.[421]

- **Failing to cooperate with a contractor**: (1) Government limited
  the number of security clearances available for civilian employees
  of a security service contractor, thereby requiring the contractor to
  pay overtime wages in order to staff the required posts.[422]

---

[416] *Hol-Gar Mfg. Corp. v. United States*, 360 F.2d 634, 175 Ct. Cl. 518
(1966).

[417] *Elas Pamfilis Painting Co.*, ASBCA No. 30113, 86-2 BCA ¶ 18,913.

[418] *Baltimore Contractors Inc. v. United States*, 12 Cl. Ct. 328 (1987).

[419] *Bill Wright Painting & Decorating Inc.*, ASBCA No. 33343, 87-1 BCA
¶ 19,666.

[420] *Harris System Int'l, Inc.*, ASBCA No. 33280 88-2 BCA ¶ 20,641.

[421] *R.W. Contracting, Inc.*, ASBCA No. 24627, 84-2 BCA ¶ 17,302.

[422] *Old Dominion Security*, ASBCA No. 40062, 91-3 BCA ¶ 24,173.

(2) Government failed to properly communicate with computer survey contractor by not informing contractor during negotiation and preaward survey that the contractor's proposed system would have to be extensively modified to meet survey requirements, even though the Government knew this.[423] (3) Government breached its duty to cooperate in the repair of a broken sewer line by failing to timely reduce water pressure to levels that permitted repair.[424]

• **Failure to disclose superior knowledge**: (1) Government failed to disclose knowledge about performance, costs, and duration of required work.[425] (2) Government withheld information in its possession that was not available to a contractor that showed that (i) a brand name component required by the contract was still in the developmental stage; (ii) there was no software data available; and (iii) there was no likelihood of timely availability of hardware and software for the brand name component.[426]

• **Constructive acceleration**: (1) Government refused to grant excusable delay for unusual and severe weather conditions that caused closure of a river on which coal was shipped by barge.[427] (2) Government accelerated a contract for a heat distribution system by establishing an extracontractual interim completion date.[428]

Under the Changes clause, a request for an equitable adjustment may be made for constructive changes as well as formal ones:

If any such change causes an increase or decrease in the cost of, or the time required for, performance of any part of the work under this contract, *whether or not changed by the order*, the contracting officer shall make an

---

[423] *Automated Servs. Inc.*, GSBCA No. EEOC-2, 81-2 BCA ¶ 15,303.

[424] *James Lowe, Inc.*, ASBCA No. 42026, 92-2 BCA ¶ 24,835.

[425] *Petrochem Servs. Inc. v. United States*, 837 F.2d 1076 (Fed. Cir. 1988); *Chemical Technology Inc. v. United States* 645 F.2d 934, 227 Ct. Cl. 120 (1981).

[426] *Lear Siegler, Inc.*, ASBCA No. 16079, 73-1 BCA ¶ 10,004.

[427] *Alley-Cassetty Coal Co.*, ASBCA No. 33315, 89-3 BCA ¶ 21,964.

[428] *Hurst Excavating Inc.*, ASBCA No. 37351, 93-3 BCA ¶ 25,935.

equitable adjustment in the contract price, the delivery schedule or both, and shall modify the contract (emphasis added).[429]

For each change made, the contractor should document the change and notify the contracting officer of a potential equitable adjustment.

3. Constructive Changes

In the case of a constructive change, the contractor is responsible for alerting the contracting officer of the change in writing and giving written notice if there will likely be a request for an equitable adjustment. Only through vigilant policing of all changes, whether initiated by the contracting officer or any member of the contracting officer's team, can the contractor be assured of receiving everything it is legally entitled to receive.

4. Mandatory Notice

A contractor's intent to request an equitable adjustment is just one of many situations that give rise to a notice requirement. The contractor must review every clause in the contract in order to know precisely where the other mandatory-notice provisions fall and then provide such notice as appropriate. Contractors often find it useful to create a checklist of these clauses for each contract. Some typical notice requirements are found in clauses relating to:

- differing site conditions[430] (in construction contracts, failure to provide prompt written notice of the differing conditions negates a request for an equitable adjustment);

- suspension of work[431] (within 20 days for a constructive suspension);

---

[429] FAR 52.243-1(b).

[430] FAR 52.236-2.

[431] FAR 52.242-14.

- stop work[432] (within 30 days after the end of the period of work stoppage);

- Government delay of work[433] (within 20 days for a constructive delay); and

- changes (30-day requirement as previously discussed).

B. Impracticability or Mistake

Contractors can obtain relief because of impracticability (impossibility) of performance or because of mutual mistake when the contract was formed. In the case of impracticability, the contractor may be relieved of performance where (1) circumstances change drastically between the time of award and there is no indication that the contractor assumed this risk; or (2) it is impracticable for a reason that the contractor did not know and had no way of knowing when the contract was formed. This type of relief is *not* available where the contractor lacked the basic ability to perform the contract (i.e., was not competent).

If the contractor and the Government make a mutual mistake of a basic assumption (i.e., a factual issue) relating to the contract, or the contractor has made a unilateral mistake but the Government should have known of it (e.g., the contractor made a mathematical error or misread the specifications), the contractor may be able to obtain relief, if the contractor did not assume the resulting risk.

C. Delays and Accelerations

When a Government-caused delay in the contract is compensable under the Delay or Stop Work clause, the contractor should submit a claim for all appropriate additional costs. Furthermore, where a contracting officer accelerates performance, the contractor may assert a claim for the extra costs, such as additional overtime, supervision, and transportation. As with all claims, the contractor must be careful to comply with procedures for notice and claims.

---

[432] FAR 52.242-15.

[433] FAR 52.242-17.

D. Requests for Equitable Adjustments

The standard FAR clauses call for an equitable adjustment, upward or downward, in the event that some occurrence such as a change, differing site condition, defective or late Government property, or issuance of a stop-work order, causes an increase or decrease in the contractor's cost of performance of the work. The most difficult task with equitable adjustments is proving the amount of the adjustment. The burden of proof is on the party that is claiming the benefit of the adjustment.

A request for equitable adjustment is considered a nonroutine request for payment and need not be the subject of a preexisting disagreement to qualify as a claim under the Contract Disputes Act ("CDA").[434] Thus, a contractor has a choice. It can submit a request for equitable adjustment ("REA") to the contracting officer—calling for a negotiated settlement—or of submitting a CDA claim requesting a contracting officer decision and starting the running of interest. Many contractors submit their initial request as a proposal rather than as a claim in order to facilitate a negotiated settlement. Under this approach, costs incurred during the negotiation process will be considered administration costs and will most likely be allowable costs. A disadvantage of this approach is that contractors forgo the commencement of interest on a claim. Another reason for submitting an REA as a proposal rather than a claim is that the submission of a claim may chill negotiations. If the contracting officer does not act on the proposal or there is a breakdown in negotiations, then the contractor has to submit a claim. Generally the necessary steps to covert the REA proposal into a claim is requesting a contracting officer's final decision and certifying the claim, if it is over the $100,000 threshold.

E. Volunteerism

Volunteers embark upon duties of their own free will and without any expectation that they will be paid for the work, and Government contractors sometimes unwittingly fall into this category. If a contractor freely elects to perform work not required by a contract and without a formal change order, the contractor is a volunteer that will not be paid for the services.[435] Contrac-

---

[434] *Reflectone, Inc. v. Dalton*, 60 F.3d 1572 (Fed. Cir. 1995).

[435] *North Star Alaska Hous. Corp. v. United States*, 30 Fed. Cl. 259, 272 (1993), citing *Calfon Constr. v. United States*, 17 Cl. Ct. 171, 177 (1989).

tors should be wary of any situation where the Government asks for services or performance not included in the contract. To be compensated for such a constructive change, the contractor must identify the work, notify the contracting officer, and request an appropriate change order and equitable adjustment. If the contracting officer refuses, the contractor should not perform the work unless it intends to be a volunteer and perform uncompensated work.

F. Assertion of Claim

The submission of a claim initiates the disputes process. A contractor's claim triggers the contracting officer's obligation to make a timely decision,[436] and begins the running of interest.[437] All claims by a contractor against the Government relating to a contract must be in writing and must be submitted to the contracting officer for a decision.[438]

1. Requirements of Claim

In order to comply with the Contract Disputes Act of 1978,[439] the FAR,[440] and a court decision,[441] a claim must meet specific requirements. The claim must:

1. be in writing;

2. request a final decision from the contracting officer;

3. seek payment as a "matter of right";

4. seek a sum certain (an exact amount);

---

[436] 41 U.S.C. § 605(c).

[437] 41 U.S.C. § 611.

[438] 41 U.S.C. § 605(a).

[439] 41 U.S.C. §§ 601–613.

[440] FAR 33.201.

[441] *Reflectone, Inc. v. Dalton*, 60 F.3d 1572 (Fed. Cir. 1995).

5. be made with specificity;

6. be certified, if the claim is over $100,000;[442]

7. be submitted to the contracting officer; and

8. be nonroutine (or in dispute), i.e., not be an invoice, voucher, or other routine request for payment that was not in dispute when submitted.

The following six elements should be included in documenting the claim:

1. summary of the claim;

2. discussion of the relevant contract requirements;

3. explanation of the actual work performed (or how work was impeded);

4. outline of extra or changed work forming the basis of the claim;

5. pricing/computation of the amount of the claim; and

6. legal basis or theory for the claim.

Of course, claims and equitable adjustments should be priced accurately and completely. The contractor's written work (probably a spreadsheet with some type of backup attached) should be self-explanatory to an auditor or a cost and price analyst.

---

[442] The certification should read as follows: "I certify that the claim is made in good faith; that the supporting data are accurate and complete to the best of my knowledge and belief; that the amount requested accurately reflects the contract adjustment for which the contractor believes the Government is liable; and that I am duly authorized to certify the claim on behalf of the contractor." FAR 33.207.

A claim must be submitted within six years after the accrual of the claim.[443] The Act does not define what constitutes the "accrual" of a claim.

2. *Final Decision of the Contracting Officer*

Once a contractor asserts a claim, the CDA requires the issuance of a final decision.[444] A contracting officer is required to issue a decision "on any submitted claim of $100,000 or less within sixty days from his receipt of a written request from the contractor that a decision be rendered within that period."[445] For claims over $100,000, a contracting officer must, within sixty days of receipt, issue a decision or notify the contractor of the time within which a decision will be issued.[446]

If the contracting officer fails to issue a timely decision the contractor may request that the agency board or the Court of Federal Claims order the contracting officer to make a decision.[447] If a contractor requests that the board or court "order" the contracting officer to issue a decision, the case is not regarded as an appeal on the merits but merely the request for an order to issue a decision. Once a contracting officer's final decision is issued, the contractor must file a new appeal if it wants to challenge the decision. Alternatively, when the contracting officer does not issue a timely decision, a contractor may appeal a "deemed denied" decision.[448] For claims of $100,000 or less, a contractor may immediately appeal once a contracting officer has failed to issue a decision within the prescribed 60-day period. If a contractor files an appeal before the expiration of 60 days, it will be found to be premature.[449] For claims exceeding $100,000, a claim will not be deemed

---

[443] 41 U.S.C. § 605(a).

[444] 41 U.S.C. § 605(b).

[445] 41 U.S.C. § 605(c).

[446] 41 U.S.C. § 605(c)(2).

[447] 41 U.S.C. § 605(c)(4).

[448] 41 U.S.C. § 605(c)(5). Note that these provisions only apply to decisions on contractor claims. The board cannot direct issuance of a final decision on a Government claim. *McDonnell Douglas Corp. v. United States*, 754 F.2d 365 (Fed. Cir. 1985).

[449] *Max Castle*, AGBCA No. 97-128-1, 97-1 BCA ¶ 28,833.

denied until a reasonable time to issue the contracting officer's decision has expired.[450]

G. Litigation at the Boards and Courts

Once a contracting officer issues a decision on a claim, that decision may be appealed to either an agency board of contract appeals or the Court of Federal Claims.[451]

1. Boards of Contract Appeals

There are eleven boards of contract appeals located in the following agencies: Agriculture, Armed Services (Defense), Transportation, Energy, General Services Administration, Housing & Urban Development, Interior, Labor, Postal Service, Veterans Affairs, and the Government Printing Office. Agencies without a board use another board under cross-servicing arrangements.[452] The appeals boards conduct trials at locations most convenient to the parties. Usually a single administrative judge hears the case and writes the decision. Subsequently, this decision is adopted by a panel of three to five judges as the decision of the full board. Although the agency boards of contract appeals are administrative bodies, the boards provide full due process including discovery and trial-type hearings.

In an effort to promote efficiency there is an "accelerated" procedure for handling claims of $100,000 or less,[453] and an "expedited" procedure for

---

[450] *Defense Sys. Co.*, ASBCA No. 50534, 97-2 BCA ¶ 28,981.

[451] In addition, the U.S. district courts may also award declaratory and injunctive relief. 28 U.S.C. § 1491(b)(2). Under the Tucker Act, the U.S. district courts may award monetary remedies only up to $10,000. 28 U.S.C. § 1346(a)(2). Recently, the U.S. district courts were given authority to award monetary damages greater than $10,000 under the Administrative Dispute Resolution Act. 28 U.S.C. § 1491(b).

[452] For example, the Department of Health and Human Services uses the Armed Services Board of Contract Appeals; the Commerce and Treasury Departments use the General Services Administration Board of Contract Appeals.

[453] 41 U.S.C. § 607(f).

claims of $50,000 or less.[454] Both procedures are available solely at the election of the contractor. Under the accelerated procedure, the board is required to make a decision, "whenever possible, within 180 days from the date the contractor elects to utilize such procedure," and "appeals under the small claims procedure shall be resolved, whenever possible, within 120 days from the date the contractor elects to utilize such procedure." The boards have also adopted alternative disputes resolution ("ADR") procedures in an effort to enhance the efficiency of the appeals process. The ADR procedures most commonly available are settlement judges, mini-trials, and summary trials with binding decisions.

2. Court of Federal Claims

Congress established the U.S. Court of Claims in 1855 to handle claims against the Federal Government. The court was renamed the Court of Federal Claims by the Federal Courts Administration Act of 1992.[455] The Court of Federal Claims is composed of sixteen judges, appointed for fifteen-year terms by the President. As Article I judges, the Court of Federal Claims judges are vested with authority to "enter dispositive judgments," including orders on dispositive motions. The proceedings of the Court of Federal Claims are conducted according to the Federal Rules of Evidence.[456] The court is not bound by the Federal Rules of Civil Procedure, but it has incorporated them in its own rules "to the extent appropriate for proceedings in this court."[457]

The Court of Federal Claims is located in Washington, D.C. and may hold a trial at any location depending upon the convenience of the parties and witnesses.[458] Cases before the Court of Federal Claims are heard and decided by one judge.[459] The decisions of the predecessor court, the Court of Claims, are regarded as binding precedent.[460] Conflicts between the deci-

---

[454] 41 U.S.C. § 608(a).

[455] Pub. L. No. 102-572.

[456] 28 U.S.C. § 2503(b).

[457] RCFC Preamble (May 1, 2002).

[458] 28 U.S.C. § 173.

[459] 28 U.S.C. § 174(a).

[460] *South Corp. v. United States*, 690 F.2d 1368 (Fed. Cir. 1982).

sions of individual judges on the court are resolved by the Court of Appeals for the Federal Circuit.[461]

3. Court of Appeals for the Federal Circuit

The Court of Appeals for the Federal Circuit hears appeals directly from both agency board decisions and Court of Federal Claims decisions, pursuant to their respective CDA jurisdictions. When appealing a board decision, the Government or contractor has 120 days to file with the court.[462] Appeals from the Court of Federal Claims must be received by the clerk of the court within 60 days of entry of the Court of Federal Claims' judgment.

H. Summary: Rules for Special Administrative Matters

1.   Take direction only from Government officials with actual authority (primarily the contracting officer), and have the direction confirmed in writing.

2.   Read and interpret the requirements of the contract as a whole.

3.   Follow design specifications exactly and immediately advise the contracting officer if they are defective.

4.   Upon finding either impracticability or some mutual mistake in the contract, alert the contracting officer immediately.

5.   Cooperate with the Government in the performance of the contract (remembering that the Government, too, is required to cooperate).

6.   Comply with all Government-ordered changes that are within the scope of the contract.

---

[461] *West Coast General Corp. v. Dalton*, 39 F.3d 315 (1994) (Court of Federal Claims decisions do not set binding precedent for separate and distinct cases in that court).

[462] 41 U.S.C. § 607(g)(1).

7.   Insist that all modifications to the contract be made in writing and signed by a person with proper authority.

8.   Keep track in writing of all constructive changes and immediately notify the contracting office of such changes, especially if they are ordered by someone other than the contracting officer.

9.   Provide all required notices to the contracting office, such as notices of intent to request an equitable adjustment or to file a claim.

10. Seek appropriate compensation for all qualifying Government delays or accelerations.

11. Do not be a volunteer.

12. Verify that all claims comply with the regulations and prepare claims and requests for equitable adjustments carefully and accurately.

13. Comply with the rules of the boards of contract appeals, the U.S. Court of Federal Claims and the U.S. Court of Appeals for the Federal Circuit.

IV. TERMINATIONS

A. Termination for Default

The Default clause that will be included in the contract states that the Government has the right to terminate a contract completely or partially for default if the contractor fails to (1) make delivery of supplies or perform services within the time specified in the contract; (2) perform any other provision of the contract; or (3) make progress and that failure endangers performance of the contract.[463] Termination for default comes with grave and far-reaching consequences. It effectively places a "black mark" on the contractor's past performance record that severely hamper the contractor in winning future contract awards. It subjects the contractor to financial penalties, including contract loss and a likely bill from the Government for

---

[463] FAR 52.249-8.

"excess costs of reprocurement," that is, any additional cost that the Government incurs when it replaces the defaulted contract with a new contract. Upon receiving an indication that a contract is in danger of being terminated for default, the contractor must take immediate action to prevent the default.

Normally, the Government will issue a Cure Notice to the contractor specifying the failure to perform and giving the contractor 10 days to cure the failure. If the contractor has failed to deliver an item on time, the Government need not give any time to cure; it may simply issue a Show Cause notice which places on the contractor the burden of demonstrating why the contract should not be defaulted. Upon receiving either a Cure or Show Cause notice,[464] the contractor should respond to the contracting

---

[464] FAR 49.607 provides that:

CURE NOTICE

You are notified that the Government considers your ... [specify the contractor's failure or failures] a condition that is endangering performance of the contract. Therefore, unless this condition is cured within 10 days after receipt of this notice [or insert any longer time that the Contracting Officer may consider reasonably necessary], the Government may terminate for default under the terms and conditions of the ... [insert clause title] clause of this contract.

If the time remaining in the contract delivery schedule is not sufficient to permit a realistic "cure" period of 10 days or more, the following "Show Cause Notice" may be used. It should be sent immediately upon expiration of the delivery period.

SHOW CAUSE NOTICE

Since you have failed to ... [insert "perform Contract No. ... within the time required by its terms", or "cure the conditions endangering performance under Contract No. ... as described to you in the Government's letter of ..... (date)"], the Government is considering terminating the contract under the provisions for default of this contract. Pending a final decision in this matter, it will be necessary to determine whether your failure to perform arose from causes beyond your control and without fault or negligence on your part. Accordingly, you are given the opportunity to present, in writing, any facts bearing on the question to .... [insert the name and complete address of the contracting officer], within 10 days after receipt of this notice. Your failure to present any excuses within this time may be considered as an admission that none exist. Your attention is invited to the respective rights of the Contractor and the Government and the liabilities that may be invoked if a decision is made to terminate for default.

Any assistance given to you on this contract or any acceptance by the Government of delinquent goods or services will be solely for the purpose of mitigating damages, and it is not the intention of the Government to condone any delinquency or to waive any rights the Government has under the contract.

officer immediately *in writing*. This correspondence should provide substantial and detailed reasons why default is inappropriate, including legal reasons from the contractor's counsel. Indeed, the entire response should be coordinated and prepared through counsel. In addition to furnishing a written document to the contracting officer, the contractor should request that the contracting officer take no action until a meeting between the contractor and contracting officer can take place and the contractor can personally make its case. If all else fails, the contractor should ask the contracting officer to consider options other than default. These include partial termination, termination for convenience, and no-cost termination settlements.[465]

After doing everything possible to prevent a default termination, the contractor should be prepared to take an appeal to either the Court of Federal Claims or the appropriate board of contract appeals. This is formal litigation, and it should be undertaken only with the assistance of Government contracts counsel. Essentially, the contractor will attempt to show that the contracting officer had no basis or an improper basis for the default termination, and that the default termination was improper. If the contractor wins, the termination for default will be converted to a termination for the convenience of the Government.[466] This outcome has two advantages: the contractor will recover all costs incurred in performing the contract prior to the default plus profit, and the "black mark" of default will be expunged from the contractor's performance record.

B. Termination for Convenience of the Government

Termination for the convenience of the Government is a unique clause in Government contracts, for it grants the Government the unilateral right to terminate the contract in whole, or from time to time, whenever such a termination is "in the Government's interest."[467] The purpose of termination for convenience is to allow the Government to take into consideration, for example, significant changes in its requirements, lack of appropriated funds by Congress, the end of wars, or natural disasters.

---

[465] *See, e.g.,* FAR 49.402-4.

[466] FAR 49.401 and FAR 52.249-8(g).

[467] FAR 52.249-2(a).

If a contract is terminated for convenience, the contractor is required to close out the contract efficiently, conclude all work, and submit a proposed termination settlement within one year. The contractor is entitled to include in the settlement all costs of work performed, plus a reasonable allowance for profit on the work actually performed, but no additional profit (i.e., profits anticipated from the complete performance of the entire contract). Unlike allowable costs under a cost-reimbursement contract, the purpose of a settlement proposal is to compensate the contractor fairly for work done. This is a matter of judgment; it is not totally subject to the cost principles in the FAR and it cannot be measured precisely.[468] The FAR encourages use of estimated data in addition to the normal cost and accounting data and recognizes that fair compensation for a convenience termination may be difficult. The contractor's reasonable costs of preparing the settlement proposal are also allowed.[469]

The contractor should submit a timely settlement proposal, discuss it with the contracting officer, point out the flexibility granted to the contracting officer in the FAR, and make a significant effort to avoid litigation. Only if the settlement proposal is unacceptable should the contractor appeal the amount to the relevant board of contract appeals or the Court of Federal Claims.

C. Summary: Rules for Contract Termination

1. If a contract is in danger of being terminated for default, take immediate action to prevent the default.

2. Appeal wrongful default terminations to the Court of Federal Claims or the appropriate agency board of contract appeals.

3. If the contract is terminated for the convenience of the Government, conclude work efficiently and submit a timely settlement

---

[468] FAR 49.201.

[469] FAR 52.249-2(g)(3).

proposal that includes all costs of the work performed plus a reasonable profit.

HOW TO GET A MULTIPLE AWARD SCHEDULE CONTRACT AND AVOID PITFALLS IN PERFORMANCE

By Karen R. O'Brien & Richard D. Lieberman

I. UNDERSTANDING WHAT FEDERAL SUPPLY SCHEDULES ARE ALL ABOUT

Many Government contractors or would be Government contractors have heard the terms MAS, GSA Schedule, FSS Program, and GSA Advantage!, but don't know what these terms mean, the benefits of being a Schedule contractor, the things to watch out for, the rules for pricing their product or service on the Schedule and, most significantly, how to become a Schedule contractor. This article discusses these points and more.

Federal Supply Schedules ("FSS") are a series of schedules compiled by the General Services Administration ("GSA") of commercial supplies and services that are frequently needed by Government agencies. The FSS includes both Single-Award Schedules ("SAS") and Multiple-Award Schedules ("MAS"). A Single-Award Schedule is a schedule in the FSS series in which there is only one contract made with a supplier for any given item at a stated price. There is a relatively small number of SASs. A Multiple-Award Schedule is a schedule in the FSS system that contains prices for comparable (but not necessarily identical) supplies or services being offered by more than one supplier. The MAS is the more common schedule. The GSA administers the FSS program for all commercial products and services. The GSA has delegated to the Department of Veterans Affairs authority to award schedule contracts for medical and nonperishable subsistence items.

The award process is straightforward: schedule contracts are awarded to *responsible* companies that offer commercial services or products at prices that are determined to be *fair and reasonable*. Since GSA is the agency responsible for MAS contracting, it is sometimes referred to as the GSA Schedule. Services and products can be ordered directly from GSA Schedule contractors or through GSA Advantage!, which is an electronic catalog and ordering system on the Internet that allows agencies to search through all GSA sources of supply and order products and services directly from contractors.

II. THE TYPE OF PRODUCTS AND SERVICES AVAILABLE ON THE SCHEDULES

Virtually every type of commercial product or service is on a Schedule. There are over four billion products and services on the FSS system. GSA categorizes the products and services as follows:

- Business Information Services
- Documents and Records Management
- Domestic Express Delivery Services
- Environmental Services and Products
- Furniture and Furnishings Services and Products
- General Products
- Grounds Maintenance
- Laboratory, Scientific, and Medical Services and Products
- Law Enforcement, Firefighting, and Security Services and Products
- Other Products and Services
- Professional and Management Services
- Recreation and Apparel Products and Services
- Information Technology ("IT")

Within each of these categories are subcategories. For instance, in the IT Center, equipment, services, and supplies are broken down into categories such as IT services, telecommunications equipment, cellular phones, pagers, and related services, etc.

III. SCHEDULE BUYERS

The following agencies are permitted to use the FSS Schedules: the executive agency, a federal agency, a mixed-ownership Government corporation, state and local governments,[470] and the District of Columbia. Also, contractors under cost-reimbursement contracts are permitted to buy off the schedules. GSA Schedules have an annual business volume in excess of $25 billion.

IV. ADVANTAGES OF BEING ON THE SCHEDULE

Probably the greatest advantage of being on the FSS Schedule is quick and easy identification and display of your product or service to a vast number of potential buyers, which obviously equates to increased sales opportunities. In addition, once you are on the schedule, making a "sale" is easy. The Schedule is much more streamlined than traditional Government procurements. In traditional procurements you first need to be aware of what goods or services a Government entity seeks to buy. This means combing FedBizOpps, a Government Internet site that advertises all procurements over $25,000, on a daily basis. Once you find an opportunity, you have to obtain the solicitation and submit a response. After that, more time elapses as the agency reviews the offers and conducts negotiations, if needed. Even for relatively easy and straightforward traditional transactions, the process is long. Moreover, the steps get repeated each and every time you submit a response to a solicitation. This is very different once you are on the Schedule. As explained below, a Schedule contractor only has to go through the offer, evaluation, and award phase once. Once on the schedule all a Government buyer needs to do is issue a purchase order based on your schedule contract, cite the source of funds, and the product or service should be delivered within the timeframe set forth in the Schedule. No further negotiation or competition is required.

V. HOW TO GET ON THE SCHEDULE

The first step is to identify the GSA Schedule that covers your product or service. In order to participate in the FSS Program you must respond to a *specific* solicitation. If you do not know what solicitation to obtain, you should go to FedBizOpps and search through the GSA Schedules, or contact GSA by telephone. You must then respond to the GSA Schedule solicitation

---

[470] State and local governments are permitted to use these schedules for automated data processing equipment, software, supplies, support equipment and services. 68 Fed. Reg. 24,372 (May 7, 2003), 48 C.F.R. § 7001.

by preparing a proposal. The proposal must be submitted in accordance with the Commercial Sales Practice ("CSP") Format and General Services Administration Regulation ("GSAR") Clause 552.212-70, Preparation of Offer (Multiple Award Schedule). The Standard Form 1449, Solicitation/Contract Order for Commercial Items, must accompany each solicitation. In addition to responding to the basic solicitation, you must submit two copies of your dated commercial pricelist containing the products you plan to offer. For an offer to be valid, it must be signed by an authorized person of the firm, and all appropriate certifications and representation must be completed. Your commercial pricelist must be completed in accordance with the CSP format. On the CSP form you must state whether the discounts and concessions that are being offered to the Government are equal to, or better than, the offeror's best price to any customer acquiring the same items offered under the special item number ("SIN"), regardless of quantity or terms and conditions. If the answer is "yes," you must complete the chart for the customer or customers who receive the offeror's best discount. If the answer is "no," you must complete the chart for all customers or categories of customers to which the offeror sells at a price which is equal to or better than the prices being offered to the Government under the solicitation. This includes agreements that you may have in place at the time the offer is made, and before award. You must also disclose whether there are any deviations from the disclosed discounting practices which result in better discounts/concessions or lower prices in column five of the chart (GSAR 515.804-6(c) Table 515-1).

VI. PRICING YOUR PRODUCT OR SERVICE

Before award of the contract, the contracting officer and the offeror will agree upon (1) the customer (or category of customers) that will be the basis of the award, and (2) the Government's price or discount relationship to the identified customer (or category of customers). The Price Reduction clause in a schedule contract provides: "This [price] relationship shall be maintained throughout the contract period. Any change in the contractor's commercial pricing or discount arrangement applicable to the identified customer (or category of customers) which disturbs this relationship shall constitute a price reduction." Recognize that if you give a discount or price reduction on any product or service to any customer you identify, you must offer the *same* price or discount to all schedule customers.

A. Understanding the difference between selling to the Government versus selling in the commercial sector

There is a unique set of rules and regulations to comply with when selling to the Government. Instead of a relatively straightforward contract, your contract will be about an inch thick consisting of Federal Acquisition Regulation ("FAR"), General Services Acquisition Regulation ("GSAR") and FSS clauses of terms and conditions. Some of these clauses may have a significant impact on you. For instance, FAR clause 52.215-20 is "Requirements for Cost or Pricing Data or Information Other Than Cost or Pricing Data." This clause authorizes the Government "the right to examine, at any time before initial award, books, records, documents, papers, and other directly pertinent records to verify the pricing, sales and other data related to the supplies or services proposed in order to determine the reasonableness of price(s)." The GSAR clause 552.215-7 contains a provision for examination of records by GSA. You will also be subject to some form of audit, e.g., Audit and Records—Negotiation clause at FAR 52.215-2 or FAR 52.212-5(d). This is not to be taken lightly. The defective pricing clause is another clause to understand. Defective pricing means that the cost or pricing data you submitted to the Government in connection with your proposal was inaccurate, incomplete, or noncurrent. If your pricing is defective, then the Government has a right to a downward price adjustment. There are also representations and certifications you will have to make in accordance with FAR 52.212-3. Another very important clause is FAR 52.212-4, which contains contract terms and conditions for commercial items. This clause covers such provisions as inspection/acceptance, risk of loss, disputes, delays, payment, and termination. A contractor will also be required to comply with certain clauses that are "incorporated by reference." Although these clauses are not written out in the contract, it does not mean that they are any less enforceable or effective. It is important to read all clauses that are incorporated by reference so that there are no later surprises.

VII. COMMON QUESTIONS

A. What is FedBizOpps?

FedBizOpps is a Government-wide Internet-based information system for announcing Government acquisitions. If you have a product or service and do not know what GSA Schedule solicitation to complete, you should go to www.fedbizopps.gov. You can also go to www.fss.gsa.gov/elibrary for an online source of schedules and contract award information.

<u>What are open solicitations?</u>

An open solicitation means that the solicitation is placed on FedBizOpps as a standing order with no closing dates. New offers may be submitted in response to these standing solicitations at any time. The initial term of the contract award is five years. The terms and conditions of solicitations will be updated periodically to incorporate all the latest changes resulting from recently issued acquisition letters, FAR and GSAR supplements. In addition, the Government has an option to extend the term of the contract for an additional five-year period. This is known as the "Evergreen" clause. The option cause may be exercised three times. This means that once a contractor gets on a schedule for a product or service, it can potentially be there for twenty years.

<u>Since a contractor can be on the schedule for a long period of time, may it increase or decrease its prices?</u>

Yes. The Economic Price Adjustments ("EPA") clause, GSAR 552.216-70, allows contractors to increase or decrease prices in accordance with their commercial practice. Because of the nature of open solicitations, this clause is of critical importance. There are, however, conditions on using this clause. Most significantly, a contractor may only request a price increase to be effective on or after the first twelve months of the contract period. In addition, the increase must be the result of a reissue or other modification of the contractor's commercial catalog or pricelist that was used as the basis for the contract award. No more than three increases will be considered during each succeeding twelve-month period of the contract. In order to prevent frequent requests for price increases, at least thirty days must elapse between requested increases. Finally, no increase will be permitted in the last sixty days of the contract period.

<u>Does either party have the right to cancel the contract?</u>

Yes. The GSAR clause at 552.238-73 provides that either party may cancel the contract in whole or in part by providing written notice. The cancellation will take effect thirty calendar days after the other party receives the notice of cancellation. You should understand that if a contractor elects to cancel, the Government would not reimburse the minimum guarantee, which is a part of every Schedule contract.

B. What is the guaranteed minimum?

The guaranteed minimum is the amount that the Government agrees to pay during the period of the contract. If a contractor receives total orders for less than the guaranteed minimum during the term of the contract, the Government will pay the difference between the amount ordered and the minimum. As a practical matter, a contractor should be able to sell substantially more than the minimum.

C. Can a contractor be required to reduce its prices?

Yes. The FSS contracts contain a Price Reduction clause under which the Government is entitled to receive a reduction in price (or an increase in discount) if during the term of the contract the contractor makes any changes in its discount or pricing practices that would result in a less advantageous relationship between the Government and the customer or category of customers, upon which the contract discount or price was predicated. Schedule contractors will not be required to pass on to all schedule users a price reduction or discount in some circumstances, mainly if sales were (1) to commercial customers under firm, fixed-price definite quantity contracts with specified delivery in excess of the maximum order threshold specified in the contract; (2) to federal agencies; or (3) if caused by an error in quotation or billing, provided adequate documentation is furnished by the contractor to the contracting officer.

D. What are spot reductions?

A spot reduction allows a schedule contractor to offer a one-time discount to a buying member without having to pass the discount on to the entire Federal Government.

If a schedule contractor gives one federal agency a lower price does this trigger the price reduction clause?

No. The price reduction does not apply if the lower sale was made to another federal agency. GSAR 552.238-75(d).

<u>What is the maximum order threshold?</u>

The maximum order ("MO") threshold is a level or trigger point wherein buying agencies receive additional price reductions. It is designed to enable agencies to get lower prices for orders above the threshold, i.e., quantity discounts.

E. What is a BPA and why is it necessary?

GSA requires schedule contractors to include a blanket purchase agreement ("BPA"). A BPA is a simple method of filling anticipated repetitive needs for services and products. They are accounts established with schedule contractors by customers. A BPA enables the parties to establish administrative protocols, such as on ordering, payment, and delivery terms. Because of potential volume of business, schedule contractors may offer increased discounts under a BPA than those available under the schedule contract.

<u>Is there a requirement to register on the Central Contractor Registration in order to be a Schedule contractor?</u>

In order to receive orders from the Department of Defense, DOD contractors must be registered with the Central Contractor Registration ("CCR") database. This is not difficult to do. Information on how to register is available at <u>http://www.ccr2000.com</u>.

F. What is the Industrial Funding Fee ("IFF")?

The GSA charges all contractors three-fourths of one percent of total quarterly sales reported as a fee for administering the schedule. The contractor must remit the IFF in U.S. dollars within thirty days after the end of each quarterly reporting period as established in clause GSAR 552.238-74. Offerors must include the IFF in their prices. The fee is included in the award price and reflected in the total amount charged to ordering activities. GSAR 552.238-76.

G. What special procedures exist for competition for services?

This is where things get a little tricky with schedule contracts. Special Ordering Procedures ("SOP") are a set of special procedures established by GSA for services—these procedures are not in the FAR. The procedures take precedence over the procedures in FAR 8.404(b)(2). The SOP provides, in part, that "[t]he request for quote should be provided to three (3) contractors if the proposed order is estimated to exceed the micro-purchase threshold, but not exceed the maximum order threshold. . . . After responses have been evaluated against the factors identified in the request, the order should be placed with the schedule contractor that represents the best value. (See FAR 8.404)." The problem here is that these procedures are really just suggestions for contracting officers, not mandatory or enforceable procedures. The use of nonmandatory procedures means that a contracting officer may ignore them and this may undermine the purpose of the SOP, which is to ensure some reasonable competition in services purchased off the schedule.

<u>What is the Most Favored Customer?</u>

The Most Favored Customer is the customer that is given the lowest price (i.e., the largest discount). The Government expects contractors on the FSS to sell supplies to the Government at prices not exceeding those given to a contractor's most favored customer. A Schedule contractor is subject to the price reduction clause if during the term of the contract the contractor makes any changes in its discount or pricing practices wherein the Government would not be the most favored customer.

Common Pitfalls

- <u>Failing to comply with the solicitation</u>: Every solicitation contains detailed instructions on how to prepare your offer, what to include in it, and how you can demonstrate that your product or service meets the requirements of the solicitation. If the solicitation is ambiguous or unclear, you must ask the contracting officer in writing for clarification well in advance of the closing date. It is important that you follow the solicitation *precisely*, even if you do not believe that the request is warranted. The Government will not award a schedule contract to you if you haven't supplied everything exactly as requested.

- Not responding in time: If the solicitation has a deadline, you must meet it. If you do not, your offer will not be considered by the Government. You should ensure that the offer is either hand-delivered and a receipt is obtained, or use a reliable commercial delivery service.

- Not making a serious offer: Your offer to the Government should be commercially competitive. If your prices are unreasonable or your terms unfair, when considered in light of the commercial market, you probably will not receive award of a contract.

- Not taking seriously the further negotiations and requests from the Government after you submit your offer: The Government frequently negotiates with you after you submit your offer. They may request clarifications, additional information, lower prices, changes in products, etc. You must work seriously with the Government buyer to include what the Government seeks—while at the same time being sure that you can provide it at the price included in your offer.

- Failing to give the Government the most favored customer pricing: As previously mentioned, your contract requires you to grant the Government most favored customer pricing. You must disclose your best pricing, and offer that (or more favorable prices) to the Government. If you fail to do so, your prices may be reduced under the price reduction clause.

- Failing to respond rapidly to contract requirements: Once you have a schedule contract, you will be required by GSA to post computerized pricelists and you are likely to be called upon to provide other information or details by GSA. It is very important that you cooperate with your Contracting Officer, because failure to comply with the contract may result in a default termination, which results not only in the loss of your contract, but potential damages you might owe to the Government.

- Failing to deliver acceptable goods or services on time: You must remember that schedule contracts are for commercial items, and you must be able to meet the delivery times in your schedule and furnish goods or services that meet the requirements of your contract. If you can't provide them, or provide them on time, you shouldn't offer to do so. As every order comes in for your product or service, you must fully comply with the specifications and delivery times in the contract.

- <u>Failing to fully disclose pricing data</u>: The defective pricing clause of the contract requires that you disclose "current, accurate and complete" cost and pricing data prior to the award of the contract. This means that you must provide the Government with *all* relevant data, it must be *as up to date as you have*, and it must be *accurate and contain no mistakes*. If your data isn't current, accurate or complete, you subject yourself to what may become significant price reductions. Two years *after* your contract is completed, the Government may issue a demand letter for a significant refund based on the defective pricing clause in your contract.

- <u>Failing to take audits seriously</u>: The Government has a right to audit your contract until three years after its completion. During the performance of the contract, the Government is likely to audit the IFF payments. After the contract is completed, they are likely to audit for defective pricing. When you are audited, you must provide all relevant records to the auditor and you should take the audit just as seriously as an audit of your tax return. You will need to demonstrate your full compliance with all contract requirements through the provision of your documents and records.

- <u>Failing to keep good records on your pricing</u>: Once you submit an offer in response to a solicitation, the Government has the right to examine, at any time before initial award, books, records, documents, papers, and other directly pertinent records to verify the pricing, sales and other data related to the supplies or services proposed.

- <u>Failing to market products:</u> Marketing your products to Government agencies is an essential part of having a successful contract. Just because your product or service is on the Schedule doesn't mean it will sell itself. If you write to or visit Government installations that likely have a need for your product or service you can explain why they should buy your product, and show them how easy it is to order from the Schedule.

Conclusion

Becoming a Schedule contractor is neither a mystery nor an arduous task—it simply requires a thorough understanding of the rules and completing all the paperwork. Make sure to take advantage of being a Schedule contractor. Once on the Schedule, understand that a product or service will still not sell itself. Being a successful Schedule contractor means *marketing* your Schedule products or services to buying customers. Avoid the common pitfalls of Schedule contractors.

APPENDIX B

HELPFUL INTERNET SITES FOR GOVERNMENT CONTRACTORS

---

www.FedBizOpps.gov

The Government Point of Entry ("GPE"), which announces all solicitations over $25,000 and frequently contains links to actual solicitations.

http://www.arnet.gov/

A source for many links to acquisition information. Takes you to the *Federal Acquisition Regulation*, a Virtual Library for contracting, business opportunities, professional development, Congressional testimony, and other resources.

http://www.arnet.gov/far/

The Official Federal Acquisition Regulation site

http://farsite.hill.af.mil/

Hill Air Force Base site containing the FAR, DFARS, DEARS and NASAFARS

http://www.acq.osd.mil/dp/

Defense Procurement home page.

http://www.gpoaccess.gov/cfr/index.html The Code of Federal Regulations